mad about
muffins
uniquely delicious muffins
anyone can make

mad about
muffins

uniquely delicious muffins
anyone can make

diana bonaparte

foulsham

LONDON • NEW YORK • TORONTO • SYDNEY

foulsham

The Publishing House, Bennetts Close, Cippenham,
Slough, Berkshire, SL1 5AP, England

Foulsham books can be found in all good bookshops and direct from www.foulsham.com

ISBN 13: 978-0-572-03198-5
ISBN 10: 0-572-03198-X

Photographs by Roger and Diana Bonaparte

A CIP record for this book is available from the British Library

The moral right of the author has been asserted

Acknowledgements
A big thank you to my husband Roger, my son Corin, my Doberman Piper and
all my family. Thank you also to Frank and Karen Kingdom and David Williams.
Another equally big thank you to Samantha and Keith Merrifield, Gill Owen and
family, Dot and Howard Greville, David and Hilary Hall, and Angus, Emma and
Jacob Hawkins. Thank you finally to everyone at W. Foulsham & Co.

Printed in China through Colorcraft Ltd., HK

CONTENTS

Introduction

'I like muffins, I like bread, All this food goes to my head!' Corin Bonaparte. Muffins are one of my son's favourite things – which is fortunate as I just love making them! It's been such fun experimenting with all kinds of ingredients for this book, from traditional chocolates, fruit and nuts to some really wild and wacky savoury options. Inspiration and experimentation are the name of the game.

A home-baked muffin is worlds away from a shop-bought one: the interior texture is light and moist, the top and the topping are crisp, and the whole thing is fresh, full of flavour and thoroughly packed with best-quality ingredients. Muffins are also really easy to make. You'll appreciate this once you have had a go yourself. They are a simple introduction to baking and would be ideal to make with children or anyone who hasn't baked before.

Muffins can be either sweet or savoury; they can be eaten on their own or as part of any meal. A soft, warm, moist muffin with its characteristic crisp top, fresh from the oven, really is something special and must be tried! As for me, I love muffins at any time, including breakfast. Most often, however, I have them for lunch and my savoury muffins also make an appearance with evening meals. Some are substantial enough to make a main meal on their own, such as my Pepperoni and Sun-dried Tomato Pizza muffins or Peanut Butter, Chilli, Coriander and Chicken muffins, for example. Others are lighter and make a perfect accompaniment to salad – just try my Goats' Cheese with Thyme or Fresh Dill with Cottage Cheese with a bowl of fresh green leaves. Muffins can also be used as bread to mop up sauces – hummus muffins in particular are great with an evening meal. Sweet muffins are wonderful just as they are, but they can be dressed up too. Remove a sweet muffin from its paper wrapper, add a dollop of ice cream (maybe with a drizzle of chocolate sauce), warm custard, softly whipped cream or even clotted cream – pure heaven!

Muffin recipes are very quick to make – most can be made, baked, eaten and washed up in an hour (wash up while the muffins are baking – this helps make the time go quicker while you are waiting!) More complex muffins – those containing fillings that need to be prepared or cooked first – may take a little longer. But don't be put off. All muffins are easy to make: just mix together the dry ingredients, mix together the wet ingredients, fold the two together and bake.

The majority of muffin recipes need only basic cooking kitchen utensils. Aside from the muffin tin and paper liners, you probably have most of these

already: scales for weighing, a sieve (strainer), a chopping board, measuring spoons, a large metal spoon, a whisk, a knife, a fork, mixing bowls, ramekins (custard cups) and a wire rack for cooling. For some recipes, you might need a few extra things, such as saucepans, a frying pan, a box grater, a vegetable peeler, a manual juicer and a baking (cookie) sheet. Other useful items include a microplane grater, a food processor, a nut or coffee grinder and a mortar and pestle. But none of these is essential.

Your muffin tin, of course, is a must! I have a standard 12-section muffin tin and a half-size 6-section tin. Both tins can be bought in good cook shops. You will find that many of my recipes make more than 12 muffins, so if you have two muffin tins, then obviously use both. If not, simply place the muffin papers into ramekins or individual pudding basins, fill with batter and bake directly on the oven rack alongside the muffin tin or on a shelf underneath. Muffins baked in a ramekin or pudding basin tend to have smooth tops, but it gets the job done and still tastes great! If you have the patience, your other option is to portion the extra batter into loose muffin paper or papers after you have filled the sections of the muffin tin, ensuring that the batter is portioned evenly. Bake the first 12 muffins in the tin, then, when they are ready, remove them and place the extra muffins, in their papers, in the tin and bake.

Muffins are at their best fresh from the oven – try to give them 10 minutes or so to cool down so you can taste all the flavours; but even cooled (at room temperature), they taste fantastic! Muffins go stale quickly, so it is best to store any leftover muffins in the freezer as soon as they have cooled to room temperature – they freeze very well. You will find that if you store sweet muffins overnight in an airtight container, the crisp top (and crunchy topping, if there was one on that particular muffin) will go soft and the muffin will be a bit stale – though this has never stopped me eating one! But to enjoy them at their very best, eat them fresh – within an hour of cooking if possible. The same applies to savoury muffins, particularly those containing meat or fish. Let them cool to room temperature and then freeze any that are not eaten straight away.

Muffins reheat successfully too. Which is great because then they are there ready for you to bring out and serve at a moment's notice! If you are in a hurry, you can just defrost a muffin in the microwave and then give it 15 seconds or so on High to warm the muffin through. However, the top will still be soft, so the best method is to defrost the muffins, then place them on a baking (cookie) sheet in a preheated oven at 180°C/350°F/gas 4/fan oven 160°C for 8–10 minutes. This way the tops go crisp again and the muffins are nice and warm.

Basic ingredients

Most of the ingredients you need to make my muffins can be found at your local supermarket. There are just a few items you may need to go to your local health food shop to buy: for example, raw red-skinned peanuts, big bags of cashew nuts, buckwheat flour, cornmeal, molasses and jumbo oats. You may also find that they are more readily available in bulk. Having bought your ingredients, it's important that you use them in the right way.

Baking powder and bicarbonate of soda (baking soda): Always use a measuring spoon and scrape the excess off the top of the spoon with a knife to get an accurate level spoonful, or weigh carefully where possible. You must measure accurately or you will get strange results and a poor taste.

Black pepper: I always use this freshly ground from the pepper mill and it should be measured once it is ground. So, if a recipe calls for a teaspoon of freshly ground black pepper, grind a teaspoonful of black peppercorns in a mortar and pestle, then use the teaspoon again to measure out the correct quantity for the recipe – quite often there is more than you need. Or you can just grind the black pepper out of the pepper mill into a small bowl and then measure it; it takes a while and your arm will ache, but it works!

Butter: I always use real butter, which gives a far better flavour than margarine. Use unsalted (sweet) only if it is stated in the recipe.

Chocolate: You will need milk (sweet), white and plain (semi-sweet) chocolate. I have found that supermarket own-brands from the baking section give perfectly good results so there is no need to buy expensive brands. Do check the percentage of cocoa solids in the plain chocolate as this affects the texture and flavour. For my recipes you will need two types – 50 per cent and 70 per cent – and I have specified which type is required in every case. You'll also use packets of plain, milk and white chocolate chips.

Coconut: I use the sweetened desiccated (shredded) variety. When it is called for as a topping, don't toast it first. If you do, it will continue to toast in the oven and come out burnt. I also use canned coconut milk – full-fat, not the low-fat variety.

Dairy products: I use semi-skimmed milk, double (heavy) cream, full-fat crème fraîche, yoghurt (either plain or Greek but not the low-fat variety of either) and buttermilk.

Dried fruit: I use the pre-soaked, ready-to-eat variety.

Fresh fruit and vegetables: Check the instructions carefully for preparing and weighing fruit and vegetables. Remember to do any chopping, dicing, peeling, etc. before you start mixing the batter.

Eggs: Always use medium size. I've based the recipes on eggs weighing 50 g/1¾ oz without their shells. For muffin recipes, you can use eggs straight from the refrigerator.

Flour: I have used both branded and store-brand plain (all-purpose) white flour and wholemeal bread flour. Cornmeal (also known as maize meal or polenta) and buckwheat flour may need to be bought at your health food shop.

Herbs: I use both fresh and dried herbs in the recipes. Check the instructions for weighing and preparation carefully.

Nuts: I buy nuts from the baking section at the supermarket or in health food shops. The nuts are shelled, either whole or in pieces (often blanched to remove skins) but still in their natural, raw state, with no salt or sugary coating. This means that you can use them whole, chopped or ground as suits the recipe. I do buy ready-ground almonds. If a recipe calls for toasted nuts, it is simple to do this yourself. Place the raw nuts on a baking (cookie) sheet and cook in a preheated oven at 180°C/350°F/gas 4/fan oven 160°C for 6–7 minutes until golden brown. Some savoury recipes are brilliant served with a handful of seaweed peanuts, which I also buy in health food shops.

Oils: Generally I use vegetable or sunflower oil – any variety that doesn't have a strong flavour. Use extra-virgin olive oil only when stated in the recipe.

Salt: I prefer to use finely ground sea salt.

Spices: I use mainly ready-ground spices, like cinnamon or paprika, but also some whole spices, such as aniseed and nutmeg, which will need to be ground or grated as stated in the recipe.

Sugar: Most of my muffin recipes use muscovado sugars. You will find both light and dark varieties widely available in supermarkets. I also use caster and granulated sugar, preferably golden varieties, and molasses sugar, a natural, unrefined cane sugar with a lovely deep flavour. I use white icing (confectioners') sugar, but you can use golden if you prefer.

Syrups: You will need golden (light corn) syrup, maple syrup, molasses (you could substitute black treacle) and clear honey.

Vanilla essence (extract): I pay the money and buy the best I can find. I also use fresh vanilla pods and, after I've split them and used the seeds, I put the empty pod in an airtight container with golden caster sugar, to make vanilla sugar. Just keep topping up both pods and sugar and you will have a continuous supply.

How to make muffins

Making muffins is really easy and you'll soon find the process becomes second nature. However, to get the very best results every time, it is worth paying attention to a few basic principles. Below I've given step-by-step instructions to making a simple muffin recipe – blueberry, in this case. Run through the steps carefully the first few times you bake until you are really familiar with the process.

1   Preheat the oven. This is **very** important, otherwise the muffins won't be properly cooked in the time stated in the recipe.

3   Start to make the batter: place a large bowl with a sieve (strainer) on top of your scales. Set the scales to zero.

2   Prepare the muffin tin. Line with paper liners or grease and flour the muffin tin sections. Prepare the exact number of muffin sections stated in each recipe.

4   Weigh all the flour, salt and sugar into the sieve.

5   Measure the raising agent. To do this accurately, fill the bowl of the measuring spoon.

8   Give the sifted dry ingredients a quick stir to be sure they are evenly mixed together.

6   Level off the excess with a knife, then add the measured quantity to the bowl. Alternatively, you can weigh the correct amount of raising agent directly into the sieve over the bowl on the scale.

9   Grate the lemon zest into the bowl.

7   Sift all the dry ingredients into the bowl.

10 Stir all the ingredients once again.

11 Beat together the eggs and buttermilk with a fork.

12 Pour the egg mixture on to the dry ingredients.

13 Add the melted butter.

14 Begin to fold the wet ingredients into the dry.

15 Scoop around the outside of the bowl with the large metal spoon, right down to the bottom of the bowl, and then bring the mixture up on top.

16 Make a couple of cutting motions across the middle of the batter, down to the bottom of the bowl.

17 This folding and cutting helps to blend the ingredients without over-mixing.

18 Stop when the flour is just moistened; the batter will be lumpy and you will still see a few floury bits.

19 Add the filling to the batter.

20 Fold the filling into the batter.

21 Use exactly the same folding and cutting method you used to mix the batter together.

22 Fold in the filling with as few folds and cuts as are necessary to distribute it evenly.

23 Spoon the batter into the prepared sections of the muffin tin. Normally, the recipes will make a sufficient quantity to fill each muffin section three-quarters full with batter.

25 Bake for the specified time. The muffins are done when they are well risen and golden and spring back when gently pressed with a finger. Remove the muffins from the tin and place on a wire rack to cool.

24 If the recipe has a topping, add it now, sprinkling it evenly over the tops.

How to prepare fresh oranges

1 Cut a slice off the top and bottom of each orange. Place the cut bottom of the orange down on the chopping board.

4 Pick it up and carefully, with your knife, cut each side of the membranes down to the centre of the orange.

2 Starting at the top of the orange and carefully following the curve of the fruit, cut away a portion of the skin, taking off all the white pith.

5 Work your way round the orange, removing the segments from the membranes.

3 Continue to do this all the way around the orange.

6 Chop the segments into pieces.

Tips for making perfect muffins

*If you have followed the step-by-step instructions in the previous chapter carefully, you should not have any problems with your muffins, and you'll enjoy some brilliant results. But because I'm a perfectionist, I'd like to give you these few extra tips to help you refine your technique. If you understand **why** you are doing something, I usually find it makes it easier to get it right every time.*

Read the whole recipe through first. Check that you have all the ingredients you need and familiarise yourself with the steps involved. You can also make sure you have enough time to make the muffin you've chosen.

Preheat the oven. The oven **must** be preheated to the temperature stated in the recipe to ensure your muffins bake properly in the time stated. Although fan ovens do not usually require preheating, I prefer to give mine a good 10 minutes – that first 'hit' in the oven is very important.

Prepare the filling ingredients before you start mixing. Sometimes you need to cook part of the filling for the muffin, soak or melt something, toast and cool some nuts and so on. It is best to do all this before you start mixing the ingredients.

Weigh and measure accurately. This is very important if you are to get best results. Almost all the ingredients in my recipes are weighed – including liquids. This follows the custom in the baking industry, where liquids are always weighed. I always measure weights in grammes as it is the most accurate method, but for very small quantities (below 5 g), I do use measuring spoons. However, the recipes include weights in both grammes and ounces, so you can use whichever you prefer – but not a mixture of both! Some items, such as fresh herbs, are difficult to measure accurately with a tablespoon, so I have given gramme weights for fresh herbs and equivalent tablespoon measurements wherever possible. These may vary from one herb to another.

Stick to the exact weights given for the filling and topping ingredients. If you use too much filling, it will all sink to the bottom and spoil the look of the finished muffin. If you use too much topping, it will disappear into the muffin, again spoiling the appearance.

Check your egg size. I use medium eggs unless otherwise stated. If you use a different size, adjust the amount of liquid or flour to obtain the right consistency

Sift the dry ingredients. This helps to make the muffins lighter and to mix the ingredients thoroughly.

Don't add extra baking powder or bicarbonate of soda (baking soda). This won't improve the texture but it will make the muffins taste funny and their tops may go all 'peaky'. Fill the bowl of the measuring spoon and level off with the back of a knife or weigh accurately. Whatever you do, don't guess.

Do add the small amount of salt. Even in sweet muffins, this heightens all the other flavours, particularly chocolate.

Don't mix the wet and dry ingredients together until you are ready to bake. By this, I mean when the oven is preheated, the muffin tin is prepared (with paper liners or greased and floured) and all your filling and/or topping ingredients are prepared (toasted, peeled and chopped) and ready to be mixed in. This is very important, because raising agents like baking powder and bicarbonate of soda (baking soda) start to work as soon as they are wet, so if you leave the mixture sitting around while you do a bit of chopping, it won't work as effectively when the batter goes into the oven and you won't get as much lift.

Don't over-mix the batter. Muffin batter should be just barely mixed. As soon as all the flour is moist, stop! It will look lumpy – this is what you want. If you need to add filling ingredients, you can stop folding the wet and dry ingredients together when you can still see just a little flour here and there in the batter. Fold your filling in with as few folds and cuts as possible. If you have over-mixed the muffin batter, the tops will be flat, you will find tunnels of air bubbles running through the muffins and the finished muffins will be dry.

Make exactly the right number of muffins. If the recipe says 14 muffins, then it means 14 muffins! If you make 12 when the recipe says 14, then the batter will overflow on to the top of the muffin tin, the finished muffins won't bake properly in the given time, will be hard to get out of the tin and will look a mess. If the recipe states 10 and you make 12, the muffins will come up small, they will be a little dry because they will have overcooked and you will be disappointed. You can still eat them, of course, but you won't get the perfect end product you were looking for!

Check your oven temperature. All ovens vary, so cooking times have to be approximate. Adjust the given cooking times and temperatures to suit your oven manufacturer's instructions and check your muffins just before the completion of the cooking time to make sure they come out perfect every time.

CHOCOLATE AND COFFEE MUFFINS

For me, coffee and chocolate are the perfect combination. Each one has a dark, mysterious, inviting smell and flavour that nothing else can match. If I haven't put them together in a muffin, then a chocolate muffin and a big mug of coffee makes a good substitute. And if there isn't a muffin, then it will be a square of dark, top-quality chocolate to be dipped briefly into my hot coffee, just to get it all starting to melt ...

In this section I'm going to tempt you with wonderfully rich, moist chocolate and coffee muffin recipes. And as well as the warm, melting chunks of white, dark and milk chocolate, I've included rich toasted nuts, spice, mint, rose, lavender, orange, ginger and even a shot of Malibu!

Remember to check the percentage of cocoa solids in your plain chocolate. It must have at least 50 per cent, in some cases 70 per cent. All the receipes specify which to use.

Chocolate and cream

This is a very simple recipe but don't be fooled. It's also stylish and sophisticated – and quite irresistible! The double cream in the batter for these delicious muffins makes the crumb centre of the finished cake especially soft and delicious to eat. A really decadent treat not to be missed!

MAKES 11 MUFFINS

FOR THE BATTER
285 g/10 oz plain (all-purpose) flour
30 g/1 oz cocoa (unsweetened chocolate) powder

1 tbsp baking powder
¹/₈ tsp salt
170 g/6 oz light muscovado sugar
100 g/3¹/₂ oz milk
190 g/6³/₄ oz double (heavy) cream

2 eggs
100 g/3¹/₂ oz butter
FOR THE FILLING
150 g/5 oz plain (semi-sweet) chocolate (70% cocoa solids), roughly chopped

1 Preheat the oven to 180°C/350°F/gas 4/fan oven 160°C. Grease and flour 11 muffin tin sections or line with paper liners.

2 Sift the dry ingredients into a large bowl, pushing the cocoa and light muscovado sugar through the sieve (strainer) with the back of a spoon.

3 Combine the milk, cream and eggs in a medium-sized bowl, mixing together with a fork without thickening the cream.

4 Melt the butter in a small bowl in the microwave or in a small saucepan.

5 Add the wet ingredients to the dry ingredients and gently fold together with a large metal spoon until just moistened.

6 Gently fold the chocolate chunks into the batter.

7 Spoon the batter into the prepared muffin tin sections.

8 Bake for 23–25 minutes until well risen and the tops spring back when gently pressed.

9 Transfer to a wire rack to cool a little before eating.

Chocolate and ginger

You'd think the amount of ginger in these muffins would blow your head off – but, trust me, it won't! My husband and my son are both ginger wimps, so I use a microplane grater to grate the stem ginger as finely as I can, but you could just chop it very finely so you get nice bits of ginger to bite into.

MAKES 12 MUFFINS

FOR THE BATTER

115 g/4 oz butter

100 g/3½ oz plain (semi-sweet) chocolate (70% cocoa solids)

2 balls of preserved stem ginger, whizzed in a food processor or finely grated

1 egg

100 g/3½ oz plain yoghurt

150 g/5 oz milk

1 tsp vanilla essence (extract)

260 g/9 oz plain (all-purpose) flour

200 g/7 oz light muscovado sugar

15 g/½ oz ground ginger

1 tsp bicarbonate of soda (baking soda)

⅛ tsp salt

FOR THE FILLING

150 g/5 oz plain chocolate (50% cocoa solids), roughly chopped

FOR THE TOPPING

1 ball of preserved stem ginger, halved and thinly sliced

1 Preheat the oven to 190°C/375°F/gas 5/fan oven 170°C. Grease and flour 12 muffin tin sections or line with paper liners.

2 Melt the butter and the chocolate together in a bowl over a pan of simmering water, stirring until smooth.

3 Add the grated stem ginger.

4 Whisk together the egg, yoghurt, milk and vanilla, then whisk this mixture into the melted chocolate and butter.

5 Sift the flour, light muscovado sugar, ground ginger, bicarbonate of soda and salt into a large bowl, pushing the light muscovado sugar through the sieve (strainer) with a spoon.

6 Add the chocolate mixture to the flour mixture and fold together until just blended.

7 Fold in the plain chocolate chunks.

8 Spoon the batter into the prepared muffin tin sections, then top each muffin with a slice of stem ginger.

9 Bake for 20–25 minutes until the muffins are well risen and the tops spring back when gently pressed.

10 Transfer to a wire rack to cool a little before eating.

Chocolate, hazelnut and chocolate chunk

This is a very satisfying muffin, full of toasted hazelnuts, chocolate chunks and a sneaky bit of molasses to intensify the chocolate and add even more depth and richness to the flavour. The nuts will only grind down to the consistency of couscous but the rough texture works well in the finished muffins.

MAKES 12 MUFFINS

FOR THE BATTER
250 g/8½ oz plain (all-purpose) flour
30 g/1 oz cocoa (unsweetened chocolate) powder
170 g/6 oz light muscovado sugar
1 tbsp baking powder

⅛ tsp salt
100 g/3½ oz hazelnuts (filberts), toasted (see page 10) and ground
170 g/6 oz milk
2 eggs
100 g/3½ oz butter
30 g/1 oz molasses

FOR THE FILLING
150 g /5 oz plain (semi-sweet) chocolate (50% cocoa solids), roughly chopped
100 g/3½ oz hazelnuts, toasted and roughly chopped

FOR THE TOPPING
50 g/1¾ oz hazelnuts, toasted and roughly chopped

1 Preheat the oven to 180°C/350°F/gas 6/fan oven 160°C. Grease and flour 12 muffin tin sections or line with paper liners.

2 Sift the flour, cocoa powder, light muscovado sugar, baking powder and salt into a large bowl, pushing the sugar through the sieve (strainer) with the back of a spoon.

3 Stir in the toasted and ground hazelnuts.

4 Combine the milk and eggs in a medium-sized bowl and mix well with a fork.

5 Melt the butter in a small bowl in the microwave or in a small saucepan. Stir the molasses into the melted butter and mix well.

6 Add the egg mixture and the butter mixture to the dry ingredients. With a large metal spoon, fold together until just moistened.

7 Gently fold in the chocolate chunks and the chopped hazelnuts.

8 Spoon the batter into the prepared muffin tin sections. Sprinkle evenly with the chopped hazelnuts.

9 Bake for 20–22 minutes until the muffins are well risen and the tops spring back when gently pressed.

10 Transfer to a wire rack to cool a little before eating.

Chocolate, orange and chocolate chunk

I'm not normally a big fan of chocolate and orange together, but I decided that millions of people – Terry included – couldn't all be wrong. So I tried it in these muffins – and I'm glad I did! So if you thought you didn't like this classic combination, give these a try and you'll be won over.

MAKES 12 MUFFINS

FOR THE BATTER
120 g/4¼ oz butter
100 g/3½ oz plain (semi-sweet) chocolate (70% cocoa solids)

2 oranges
A little milk
1 egg
1 tsp vanilla essence (extract)
285 g/10 oz plain (all-purpose) flour
200 g/7 oz light muscovado sugar

1 tsp bicarbonate of soda (baking soda)
⅛ tsp salt
FOR THE FILLING
150 g/5 oz plain chocolate (50% cocoa solids), roughly chopped

1 Preheat the oven to 190°C/375°F/gas 5/fan oven 170°C. Grease and flour 12 muffin tin sections or line with paper liners.

2 Melt the butter and the chocolate together in a bowl over a pan of simmering water until smooth.

3 Grate the zest from the oranges into a medium-sized bowl. Squeeze the juice from both fruit. Make the orange juice up to 190 g/6¾ oz with a little milk and combine with the orange zest. Add in the egg and vanilla and mix well, then whisk this mixture into the melted chocolate and butter.

4 Sift the flour, light muscovado sugar, bicarbonate of soda and salt into a large bowl. You will need to push the light muscovado sugar through the sieve (strainer) with the back of a spoon.

5 Add the butter and chocolate mixture to the flour mixture and fold everything together until just blended.

6 Fold in the chocolate chunks.

7 Spoon the batter into the prepared muffin tin sections.

8 Bake for 22–25 minutes until the muffins are well risen and the tops spring back when gently pressed.

9 Transfer to a wire rack to cool a little before eating.

Cocoa, coconut and chocolate chunk

These chocolate muffins are full of sweet coconut and melting chunks of white and dark chocolate, with a shot of Malibu to give them a real kick. If you can call a muffin handsome – and I would argue that you can – then I think these qualify. A very adult treat – and don't we all need one from time to time!

MAKES 12 MUFFINS

FOR THE BATTER

285 g/10 oz plain (all-purpose) flour

30 g/1 oz cocoa (unsweetened chocolate) powder

1 tbsp baking powder

170 g/6 oz caster (superfine) sugar

½ tsp salt

50 g/1¾ oz sweetened desiccated (shredded) coconut

2 eggs

160 g/5½ oz coconut milk

100 g/3½ oz oil

40 g/1½ oz Malibu

FOR THE FILLING

100 g/3½ oz plain (semi-sweet) chocolate (70% cocoa solids), roughly chopped

100 g/3½ oz white chocolate, roughly chopped

FOR THE TOPPING

50 g/1¾ oz sweetened desiccated coconut

1 Preheat the oven to 200°C/400°F/gas 6/fan oven 180°C. Grease and flour 12 muffin tin sections or line with paper liners.

2 Sift the flour, cocoa, baking powder, sugar and salt into a large bowl. Stir in the desiccated coconut.

3 Combine the eggs, coconut milk, oil and Malibu in a medium-sized bowl and mix with a fork.

4 Add the egg mixture to the flour mixture and fold together with a large metal spoon until just combined. Carefully fold in the chocolate chunks.

5 Spoon into the muffin tin sections, then sprinkle the coconut topping evenly over each muffin.

6 Bake for 22–24 minutes until the muffins are well risen and the tops spring back when gently pressed with a finger.

7 Transfer to a wire rack to cool a little before eating.

Coffee and cream

The double cream gives these sophisticated muffins a luscious softness to their texture that everyone will love. They smell wonderful when they are just baked – an utterly irresistible aroma – so you won't find they hang around on the plate for long. You could even try baking them if you are trying to sell your house!

MAKES 12 MUFFINS

FOR THE BATTER
300 g/10½ oz plain (all-purpose) flour
170 g/6 oz caster (superfine) sugar
1 tbsp baking powder
10 g/2 tbsp instant coffee powder or granules
⅛ tsp salt
100 g/3½ oz milk
185 g/6½ oz double (heavy) cream
100 g/3½ oz oil
2 eggs

FOR THE TOPPING
40 g/1½ oz demerara sugar

1 Preheat the oven to 180°C/350°F/gas 4/fan oven 160°C. Grease and flour 12 muffin tin sections or line with paper liners.

2 Sift the dry ingredients into a large bowl, pushing the coffee through the sieve (strainer) with the back of a spoon.

3 Combine the wet ingredients in a medium-sized bowl and mix together with a fork but try not to thicken the cream.

4 Add the wet ingredients to the dry ingredients and gently fold together with a large metal spoon until just moistened.

5 Spoon into the prepared muffin tin sections and sprinkle the tops with demerara sugar.

6 Bake for 23–25 minutes until well risen and the tops spring back when you gently press on them.

7 Transfer to a wire rack to cool a little before eating.

If you need chocolate!

I love deep, dark, intense chocolate, and I like it warm and melting – as you may have worked out by now if you've made any of my earlier recipes! These muffins satisfy all my desires and are irresistible and so easy to make! Try to give them a few moments cooling on the rack, then devour. Why fight it?

MAKES 12 MUFFINS

FOR THE BATTER

115 g/4 oz butter

100 g/3½ oz plain (semi-sweet) chocolate (70% cocoa solids)

275 g/9¾ oz plain (all-purpose) flour

200 g/7 oz light muscovado sugar

1 tsp bicarbonate of soda (baking soda)

⅛ tsp salt

1 egg

100 g/3½ oz plain yoghurt

150 g/5 oz milk

2 tsp vanilla essence (extract)

FOR THE FILLING

150 g/5 oz plain chocolate (50% cocoa solids), roughly chopped

1 Preheat the oven to 190°C/375°F/gas 5/fan oven 170°C. Grease and flour 12 muffin tin sections or line with paper liners.

2 Melt the butter and chocolate together in a bowl over a saucepan of water on a low heat. Remove from the heat.

3 Sift the flour, sugar, bicarbonate of soda and salt into a large bowl, pushing the sugar through the sieve (strainer) with the back of a spoon.

4 Whisk together the egg, yoghurt, milk and vanilla in a medium-sized bowl. Then whisk the egg mixture into the melted chocolate and butter.

5 Fold the chocolate mixture into the flour with a large metal spoon until just blended, then fold in the chocolate chunks.

6 Spoon the batter evenly into the muffin tin sections.

7 Bake for 22–25 minutes until the muffins are well risen and spring back when you gently press them – but watch out for hot, melted chocolate chunks!

8 Transfer to a wire rack to cool a little before eating.

If you need chocolate with toasted pecans

Oh, just the thought – warm, dark chocolate muffin, melting chocolate chunks and toasted pecans! When I eat this muffin, I like to prise it in half so I can see all the melted chocolate chunks and pieces of pecans running through the middle. So I often buy extra pecans and place two whole pecans on top of each muffin – that way I get a whole pecan on top of each half.

MAKES 15 MUFFINS

FOR THE BATTER
115 g/4 oz butter
100 g/3½ oz plain (semi-sweet) chocolate (70% cocoa solids)
275 g/9¾ oz plain (all-purpose) flour

200 g/7 oz light muscovado sugar
1 tsp bicarbonate of soda (baking soda)
⅛ tsp salt
1 egg
100 g/3½ oz plain yoghurt
150 g/5 oz milk
2 tsp vanilla essence (extract)

FOR THE FILLING
200 g/7 oz plain chocolate (50% cocoa solids), roughly chopped
150 g/4¼ oz pecan nuts, toasted (see page 10) and roughly chopped

FOR THE TOPPING
15 whole pecans (about 25 g/1 oz)

1 Preheat the oven to 180°C/350°F/gas 4/fan oven 160°C. Grease and flour 15 muffin tin sections or line with paper liners.

2 Melt the butter and the chocolate together in a bowl over a saucepan of water on a low heat. Remove from the heat.

3 Sift the flour, sugar, bicarbonate of soda and salt into a large bowl, pushing the light muscovado sugar through the sieve (strainer) with the back of a spoon.

4 In a medium-sized bowl, whisk together, the egg, yoghurt, milk and vanilla, then, whisk this mixture into the melted chocolate and butter.

5 Fold the chocolate mixture into the flour with a large metal spoon until just blended, and then fold in the plain chocolate chunks and the toasted pecans.

6 Spoon the batter into the prepared muffin tin sections. Top each muffin with a whole, untoasted pecan.

7 Bake for 22–25 minutes until the muffins are well risen and spring back when gently pressed.

8 Transfer to a wire rack to cool a little before eating.

Milk chocolate chunk

I surprised myself when I created this recipe. I love deep, dark chocolate, but I gave some milk chocolate a try in these muffins and I really enjoyed them! It just goes to show you should try new things sometimes. To my mind, they taste a bit like American chocolate chip cookies but obviously with a soft, muffin texture.

MAKES 11 MUFFINS

FOR THE BATTER
400 g/14 oz plain (all-purpose) flour
1 tbsp baking powder

$\frac{1}{8}$ tsp salt
170 g/6 oz light muscovado sugar
100 g/3½ oz butter
185 g/6½ oz milk
2 eggs

1 tsp vanilla essence (extract)
FOR THE FILLING
150 g/5 oz milk (sweet) chocolate,
    roughly chopped

1   Preheat the oven to 180°C/350°F/gas 4/fan oven 160°C. Grease and flour 11 muffin tin sections or line with paper liners.

2   Sift the dry ingredients into a large bowl and stir thoroughly, pushing the light muscovado sugar through the sieve (strainer) with the back of a spoon.

3   Melt the butter in a small bowl in the microwave or in a small saucepan.

4   In a medium-sized bowl, beat together the milk, eggs and vanilla with a fork.

5   Add the wet ingredients to the dry and gently fold together with a large metal spoon until just moistened.

6   Gently fold in the milk chocolate chunks.

7   Spoon the batter evenly into the muffin tin sections.

8   Bake for 22–25 minutes until the muffins are well risen and golden. The tops of the muffins will spring back when you press them gently.

9   Transfer to a wire rack to cool a little before eating.

Milk chocolate chunk and macadamia nut

First let me apologise – these muffins are expensive to make. However, I think the reward of the golden, buttery nuttiness, highlighted with chunks of milk chocolate, is well worth the extra cost! Save them for special occasions, if you prefer, but whenever you eat them I'm sure you won't be disappointed.

MAKES 10 MUFFINS

FOR THE BATTER
270 g/9¹/₂ oz plain (all–purpose) flour
170 g/6 oz caster (superfine) sugar
1 tbsp baking powder
¹/₈ tsp salt

100 g/3¹/₂ oz macadamia nuts, toasted (see page 10) and ground
170 g/6 oz milk
2 eggs
100 g/3¹/₂ oz butter

FOR THE FILLING
150 g/5 oz milk (sweet) chocolate, roughly chopped

100 g/3¹/₂ oz macadamia nuts, toasted and roughly chopped

FOR THE TOPPING
50 g/1³/₄ oz macadamia nuts, toasted and roughly chopped

1 Preheat the oven to 200°C/400°F/gas 6/fan oven 180°C. Grease and flour 10 muffin tin sections or line with paper liners.

2 Sift the flour, sugar, baking powder and salt into a large bowl, then stir in the ground nuts.

3 Combine the milk and eggs in a medium-sized bowl, mixing well with a fork.

4 Melt the butter in a small bowl in the microwave or in a small saucepan.

5 Add the egg mixture and the melted butter to the flour mixture. With a large metal spoon, fold together until just moistened.

6 Gently fold in the milk chocolate chunks and the chopped macadamia nuts for the filling.

7 Spoon the batter into the prepared muffin tin. Sprinkle evenly with the chopped nuts.

8 Bake for 20–23 minutes until the muffins are well risen and golden and the tops spring back when gently pressed.

9 Transfer to a wire rack to cool before eating.

Milk chocolate multi-chip

I have to thank my son Corin for this muffin. He wanted a lighter chocolate muffin with multi-coloured chocolate chips and a big dollop of white chocolate on the top! While the muffins are still warm, he likes to break off pieces from the bottom of the muffin and dip them into the white chocolate dollop. This is a really fun, messy muffin to eat warm.

MAKES 12 MUFFINS

FOR THE BATTER
115 g/4 oz butter
100 g/3½ oz milk (sweet) chocolate
275 g/9¾ oz plain (all-purpose) flour
200 g/7 oz caster (superfine) sugar
1 tsp bicarbonate of soda (baking soda)

⅛ tsp salt
1 egg
100 g/3½ oz plain yoghurt
150 g/5 oz milk
2 tsp vanilla essence (extract)
FOR THE FILLING
40 g/1½ oz plain (semi-sweet) chocolate
chips

40 g/1½ oz milk chocolate chips
100 g/3½ oz white chocolate chips
FOR THE FIRST TOPPING
60 g/2 oz plain chocolate chips
60 g/2 oz milk chocolate chips
FOR THE SECOND TOPPING
100 g/3½ oz white chocolate, melted

1 Preheat the oven to 190°C/375°F/gas 5/fan oven 170°C. Grease and flour 12 muffin tin sections or line with paper liners.

2 Melt the butter and milk chocolate together in a bowl over a saucepan of water on a low heat. Remove from the heat.

3 Sift the flour, sugar, bicarbonate of soda, and salt into a large bowl and stir well.

4 In a medium-sized bowl, whisk together the egg, yoghurt, milk and vanilla essence, then whisk this mixture into the chocolate and butter.

5 Fold the chocolate mixture into the flour until just blended. Fold in all the filling ingredients.

6 Spoon the batter into the prepared muffin tin sections.

7 Sprinkle the first topping ingredients evenly over the muffins.

8 Bake for 22–25 minutes until the muffins are well risen and they spring back when you press them gently – watch out for the hot chocolate chips on top.

9 Transfer to a wire rack to cool a little.

10 Melt the white chocolate for the second topping while the muffins are cooling. Use an ordinary teaspoon to carefully dollop the white chocolate on top of each muffin.

Mint chocolate chip

Any muffin with chocolate chips all over its surface is going to be very messy to eat while still warm – but so very delicious! As with mint chocolate chip ice-cream, these muffins had to be green too. You see the green, you see the chips, and instantly you make the connection – mint chocolate chip!

MAKES 11 MUFFINS

FOR THE BATTER
340 g/12 oz plain (all-purpose) flour
1 tbsp baking powder
1/8 tsp salt

185 g/6¹/₂ oz caster (superfine) sugar
2 eggs
190 g/6³/₄ oz milk
1 tsp peppermint essence (extract)
1 tsp green food colouring
100 g/3¹/₂ oz unsalted (sweet) butter

FOR THE FILLING
100 g/3¹/₂ oz plain (semi-sweet) chocolate chips
FOR THE TOPPING
100 g/3¹/₂ oz plain chocolate chips

1 Preheat the oven to 200°C/400°F/gas 6/fan oven 180°C. Grease and flour 11 muffin tin sections or line with paper liners.

2 Sift all the dry ingredients into a large bowl and stir well.

3 Combine the eggs, milk, peppermint essence and green food colouring in a medium-sized bowl. Beat together with a fork.

4 Melt the butter in a small bowl in the microwave or in a small saucepan.

5 Add all the wet ingredients, including the melted butter, to the dry ingredients and stir with a large metal spoon until just combined.

6 Gently fold the chocolate chips into the batter.

7 Spoon the batter into the prepared muffin tin sections. Sprinkle evenly with the topping.

8 Bake for 20–23 minutes until well risen and golden and the tops spring back when lightly pressed. Watch out for the chips – they get really hot!

9 Transfer to a wire rack to cool a little before eating.

Rose and chocolate chip

I let my imagination run riot when I'm developing new recipes. Chocolate chips look like perfect little kiss shapes. And what goes with kisses? – roses! What makes you feel all warm and fuzzy (well, me anyway)? – muffins! There you have another unique combination: rose and chocolate chip muffins!

MAKES 12 MUFFINS

FOR THE BATTER
375 g/13¼ oz plain (all-purpose) flour
1 tbsp baking powder
⅛ tsp salt

170 g/6 oz caster (superfine) sugar
100 g/3½ oz unsalted (sweet) butter
170 g/6 oz milk
2 eggs
2 tbsp rose essence (extract)
1 tsp pink food colouring

FOR THE FILLING
100 g/3½ oz plain (semi-sweet) chocolate chips

FOR THE TOPPING
100 g/3½ oz plain chocolate chips
20 g/¾ oz granulated sugar

1. Preheat the oven to 200°C/400°F/gas 6/fan oven 180°C. Grease and flour 12 muffin tin sections or line with paper liners.

2. Sift the dry ingredients into a large bowl and stir well.

3. Melt the butter in a small bowl in the microwave or in a small saucepan. In a medium-sized bowl, beat the milk, eggs, rose essence and pink food colouring together with a fork.

4. Add egg mixture and the melted butter to the dry ingredients. Gently fold together with a large metal spoon until just moistened.

5. Gently fold in the chocolate chips.

6. Spoon the batter into the prepared muffin tin sections. Top the muffins first with the chocolate chips and then with the sugar.

7. Bake for 20–22 minutes until well risen and the tops spring back when gently pressed.

8. Transfer to a wire rack to cool a little before eating.

Strong coffee, chocolate chunk and cream

Just look at the wonderful rich colour of these delicious muffins! Strong coffee and rich chocolate are blended together with cream give the most superb, soft, melting texture. This recipe is not one for the faint-hearted, however. These muffins pack a serious flavour punch! Go on, give yourself a treat.

MAKES 12 MUFFINS

FOR THE BATTER
285 g/10 oz plain (all-purpose) flour
15 g/^{1}/$_2$ oz instant coffee powder or
  granules

1 tbsp baking powder
^{1}/$_8$ tsp salt
170 g/6 oz light muscovado sugar
2 eggs
100 g/3^1/$_2$ oz milk
190 g/6^3/$_4$ oz double (heavy) cream

100 g/3^1/$_2$ oz butter
FOR THE FILLING
150 g/5 oz plain (semi-sweet) chocolate
  (70% cocoa solids), roughly chopped
FOR THE TOPPING
40 g/1^1/$_2$ oz demerara sugar

1. Preheat the oven to 180°C/350°F/gas 4/fan oven 160°C. Grease and flour 12 muffin tin sections or line with paper liners.

2. Sift the dry ingredients into a large bowl, pushing the coffee and light muscovado sugar through the sieve (strainer) with the back of a spoon. Stir well.

3. Combine the eggs, milk and cream in a medium-sized bowl and mix together with a fork. Try not to thicken the cream.

4. Melt the butter in a small bowl in the microwave or in a small saucepan.

5. Add the wet ingredients to the dry ingredients and gently fold together with a large metal spoon until just moistened.

6. Fold the chocolate chunks into the batter. Spoon the batter into the prepared muffin tin sections and sprinkle evenly with the topping.

7. Bake for 23–25 minutes until well risen and the tops spring back when gently pressed.

8. Transfer to a wire rack to cool a little before eating.

White chocolate and lavender

Romantic and yummy! You could use ordinary granulated sugar for the topping but lavender sugar gives it a wonderful subtle flavour and is very easy to make: just put a few sprigs of lavender in a jar of sugar, put on the lid and leave it for a few hours or overnight. An unusual and delightful variety to add to the repertoire of chocolate muffins.

MAKES 12 MUFFINS

FOR THE BATTER
370 g/13 oz plain (all-purpose) flour
170 g/6 oz caster (superfine) sugar
1 tbsp baking powder
⅛ tsp salt
1 tbsp fresh lavender florets
   or 1 tsp dried
190 g/6¾ oz milk
100 g/3½ oz oil
2 eggs

FOR THE FILLING
200 g/7 oz white chocolate, roughly
   chopped
FOR THE TOPPING
40 g/1½ oz lavender sugar

1 Preheat the oven to 180°C /350°F/gas 4/fan oven 160°C. Grease and flour 12 muffin tin sections or line with paper liners.

2 Sift the flour, sugar, baking powder and salt into a large bowl. Stir in the lavender.

3 Combine the milk, oil and eggs in a medium-sized bowl and beat together thoroughly with a fork.

4 Add the wet ingredients to the dry and fold together with a large metal spoon until just moistened. Very gently fold in the white chocolate chunks.

5 Spoon the batter into the prepared muffin tin sections and sprinkle the lavender sugar evenly over the tops.

6 Bake for 22–25 minutes until well risen and golden and the tops spring back when you gently press them.

7 Transfer to a wire rack to cool a little before eating.

FRUIT MUFFINS

Fruit muffins are absolutely beautiful: all those jewelled colours and juicy bursts of sweetness barely contained beneath a muffin's crisp top make them stunning both to look at and to eat.

Simply stirring fresh berries or dried fruits into a sweet muffin batter is a great way to make a fruity muffin, but I have taken the idea further. For this section I have chopped, grated, mashed, juiced, zested and puréed all kinds of fresh fruits as well as putting whole berries and dried fruits into a wide variety of muffin batters. The batters themselves are made with fresh custard, double cream, buttermilk and, of course, fruit juice. To these I've added ground nuts, spice, zest, coconut and in some cases even a little fruity liquor just to provide an intense echo of the fruit flavours. And to finish off, many of the muffins have tempting toppings, such as crumble, flaked almonds, slices of fruit and crunchy sugar, to complement the fillings and add even more texture.

Apple, cinnamon and custard crumble muffins

I use grated apple so that it is easy to distribute evenly through the mixture, giving you the flavours of apple and custard in each bite. Two medium apples will give you about the right quantity and you don't need to peel them – the peel adds extra flavour. You can use fresh shop-bought custard if you prefer, but do add a teaspoon of vanilla essence.

MAKES 12 MUFFINS

FOR THE CUSTARD
3 egg yolks
60 g/2 oz vanilla sugar
1 tsp cornflour (cornstarch)
285 g/10 oz whole or semi-skimmed milk
1 tsp vanilla essence (extract)

FOR THE BATTER
300 g/10½ oz plain (all-purpose) flour
1 tbsp baking powder
⅛ tsp salt
2 tsp ground cinnamon
A pinch of grated nutmeg (about 10 scrapes on a nutmeg grater)
185 g/6½ oz light muscovado sugar
2 eggs, lightly beaten
100 g/3½ oz butter, melted

FOR THE FILLING
200 g/7 oz grated unpeeled eating (dessert) apple

FOR THE TOPPING
60 g/2 oz jumbo oats
50 g/1¾ oz plain (all-purpose) flour
15 g/½ oz light muscovado sugar
¼ tsp ground cinnamon
20 g/¾ oz clear honey
25 g/1 oz butter, softened

1. Preheat the oven to 180°C/350°F/gas 4/fan oven 160°C. Grease and flour 12 muffin tin sections or line with paper liners.

2. First make the custard. Place the egg yolks, sugar and cornflour in a medium-sized bowl, then whisk until the ingredients are thoroughly mixed. Place the milk in a medium saucepan and heat over a medium heat for about 5 minutes, stirring from time to time with a heatproof rubber spatula or wooden spoon, until the milk is almost ready to boil – you will see the first few bubbles come up.

3. Grab your whisk, take the pan off the heat and take both to your bowl of well-whisked egg yolks, sugar and cornflour. Slowly pour the milk on to the egg mixture, whisking vigorously all the time, until all the milk is in the bowl with the eggs.

4 When all the milk has been added to the eggs, return the milk and egg mixture to the saucepan. Place the pan back on the medium heat and give it a final good whisk.

5 Using the rubber spatula or wooden spoon, stir the custard slowly but constantly until it thickens. This will take about 5 minutes and is usually completed just as the sauce starts to come up to the boil – you may see the odd bubble trying to break the surface. The finished custard will coat the back of the spoon.

6 Remove from the heat immediately and add the teaspoon of vanilla essence. Pour the custard back into the bowl and set aside to cool. Don't leave it undisturbed, however – give it a stir from time to time while you make up the batter.

7 Sift the dry batter ingredients into a large bowl, pushing the light muscovado sugar through the sieve (strainer) with the back of a spoon.

8 Lightly beat the eggs in a small bowl.

9 Add 210 g/7½ oz of the fresh custard, the melted butter and the beaten eggs to the dry ingredients, then gently fold together with a large metal spoon until just moistened.

10 Fold the grated apple into the muffin batter.

11 Spoon the batter into the prepared muffin tin.

12 Place all the topping ingredients in a bowl and rub together with your fingers until the mixture resembles crumbs. Sprinkle the crumble topping evenly over the muffins.

13 Bake for about 23–25 minutes until well risen and golden and the tops of the muffins spring back when gently pressed.

14 Transfer to a wire rack to cool a little before eating.

NOTE
If you make this custard to serve as an accompaniment with another dish, omit the teaspoon of vanilla essence – this is only required for the right intensity of flavour for the muffin.

Banana and coconut

I thought these might be too bland when I first had a go at the recipe, but they aren't; they are moist and sweet and both the banana and the coconut flavour come through evenly and complement each other very well. I always like muffins warm but these also taste delicious cold.

MAKES 7 MUFFINS

FOR THE BATTER
60 g/2 oz butter
100 g/3¹/₂ oz light muscovado sugar
250 g /8¹/₂ oz very ripe bananas (unpeeled weight)

1 egg, lightly beaten
¹/₂ tsp vanilla essence (extract)
120 g/4¹/₄ oz plain (all-purpose) flour
50 g/1³/₄ oz wholemeal flour
¹/₄ tsp salt
¹/₂ tsp bicarbonate of soda (baking soda)
40 g/1¹/₂ oz Malibu or very hot water

FOR THE FILLING
75 g/3 oz sweetened desiccated (shredded) coconut

FOR THE TOPPING
30 g/1 oz sweetened desiccated coconut
20 g/³/₄ oz demerara sugar

1. Preheat the oven to 180°C/350°F/gas 4/fan oven 160°C. Grease and flour 7 muffin tin sections or line with paper liners.

2. Melt the butter in a large bowl over a pan of simmering water or briefly in the microwave.

3. Add the sugar to the melted butter and mix well.

4. Peel the bananas and mash with a fork, then add them to the butter and sugar and mix well.

5. In the same bowl you mashed the bananas, beat the egg with the fork. Add the egg to the butter mixture, then stir the vanilla essence into the butter mixture.

6. In another bowl, sift together the plain flour, wholemeal flour, salt and bicarbonate of soda. Add back in any bran from the wholemeal flour that remains in the sieve (strainer).

7. Add half the flour to the butter mixture and mix well, then add the water or Malibu and mix well again. Add the remaining flour and stir well to mix.

8. Add the filling and stir well to combine.

9. Spoon the batter into the prepared muffin tin sections. Sprinkle the tops evenly with the sweetened desiccated coconut, then the demerara sugar.

10. Bake for 30–33 minutes or until the muffins are well risen and spring back when gently pressed.

11. Transfer to a wire rack to cool before eating.

Banana, chocolate and peanut butter

You know that I am enthusiastic about all my recipes, but my first bite of this muffin quite literally made me gasp, 'Oh my goodness!' – and then promptly shovel in more! 'Delicious' doesn't even come near describing them but they are very filling, so you'll have to share this batch. Whether you choose smooth or crunchy peanut butter is up to you.

MAKES 7 MUFFINS

FOR THE BATTER
50 g/1¾ oz plain (semi-sweet) chocolate (70% cocoa solids)
50 g/1¾ oz peanut butter
60 g/2 oz butter

100 g/3½ oz light muscovado sugar
250 g/8½ oz very ripe bananas (unpeeled weight)
1 egg
½ tsp vanilla essence (extract)
100 g/3½ oz plain (all-purpose) flour
50 g/1¾ oz wholemeal flour

¼ tsp salt
½ tsp bicarbonate of soda (baking soda)
35 g/1¼ oz very hot water
FOR THE FILLING
50 g/1¾ oz plain chocolate (70% cocoa solids), roughly chopped
7 tsp peanut butter

1 Melt the chocolate and peanut butter together in a small bowl over a pan of simmering water. Remove from the heat.

2 Preheat the oven to 160°C/325°F/gas 3/fan oven 140°C. Grease and flour 7 muffin tin sections or line with paper liners.

3 Melt the butter in a large bowl over a pan of simmering water or briefly in the microwave. Add the sugar and mix thoroughly.

4 Peel the bananas and mash in a medium-sized bowl. Add to the butter and sugar and mix well.

5 In the same bowl you used for the bananas, beat the egg with the fork. Add the egg to the banana mixture and stir in the vanilla.

6 Sift the flours, salt and bicarbonate of soda into a separate bowl. Tip in the bran from the wholemeal flour that stayed in the sieve (strainer).

7 Mix half the flour into the banana mixture, then add the hot water and stir well. Add the rest of the flour, stirring thoroughly again. Add the melted chocolate and peanut butter and stir thoroughly to mix. Stir in the chocolate chunks.

8 Spoon just a little of the muffin batter into each prepared section of the muffin tin, not even half filling them. Add a teaspoonful of peanut butter to the centre of each. Cover the peanut butter with the remaining batter, filling the tins evenly.

9 Bake for 30–33 minutes until the muffins are well risen and spring back when you gently press the tops.

10 Transfer to a wire rack to cool.

Banana, date and muesli crumble

These are just downright yummy and completely irresistible! You can see in the photograph opposite the wonderful textures created by oats and the seeds on the top – and you can vary the seeds you use according to what you have in your store cupboard. I'm sure you'll be experimenting with your own recipes by now.

MAKES 8 MUFFINS

FOR THE BATTER
60 g/2 oz butter
100 g/3½ oz light muscovado sugar
250 g/8½ oz very ripe bananas (unpeeled weight)
1 egg
½ tsp vanilla essence (extract)
60 g/2 oz plain (all-purpose) flour

50 g/1¾ oz wholemeal flour
½ tsp bicarbonate of soda (baking soda)
¼ tsp salt
60 g/2 oz porridge oats
35 g/1¼ oz very hot water

FOR THE FILLING
70 g/2½ oz sugar-rolled or ready-to-eat dates, chopped
30 g/1 oz sweetened desiccated (shredded) coconut

FOR THE TOPPING
50 g/1¾ oz jumbo oats
50 g/1¾ oz plain flour
10 g sunflower seeds
5 g sesame seeds
15 g/½ oz light muscovado sugar
20 g/¾ oz clear honey
30 g/1 oz butter, softened

1 Preheat the oven to 180°C/350°F/gas 4/fan oven 160°C. Grease and flour eight muffin tin sections or line with paper liners.

2 Melt the butter in a large bowl over a pan of simmering water or briefly in the microwave. Place the bowl on your work surface and add the sugar and mix thoroughly.

3 Peel the bananas and mash them in a medium-sized bowl with a fork. Add them to the butter and sugar and mix thoroughly.

4 In the same bowl you used for the bananas, beat the egg with the fork. Add to the butter mixture, then stir in the vanilla.

5 Sift the flours, bicarbonate of soda and salt into a medium-sized bowl. Tip in all the bran from the wholemeal flour that stayed in the sieve (strainer). Stir in the porridge oats.

6 Add half the flour mixture to the butter mixture and mix it in thoroughly. Add the hot water and mix it in thoroughly. Finally, mix in the remaining flour mixture.

7 Add the filling ingredients and stir thoroughly to combine.

8 Spoon the batter evenly into the sections of the muffin tin.

9 Combine and rub together the topping ingredients in a small bowl. Sprinkle evenly over the muffins.

10 Bake for 30–33 minutes or until the muffins are well risen and spring back when you gently press the tops.

11 Transfer to a wire rack to cool a little before eating.

Blackberry and white chocolate dot

I like the overall sweetness that comes from the tiny dots of white chocolate in these lovely muffins. Using white chocolate chips rather than chopped chunks gives you a more even mix of blackberry and white chocolate flavour in each bite, which I think makes the recipe work particularly well.

MAKES 12 MUFFINS

FOR THE BATTER
360 g/12³⁄₄ oz plain (all-purpose) flour
1 tbsp baking powder
¹⁄₈ tsp salt
170 g/6 oz caster (superfine) sugar
100 g/3¹⁄₂ oz butter
200 g/7 oz milk
2 eggs

1 tsp vanilla essence (extract)
FOR THE FILLING
200 g/7 oz fresh or frozen blackberries
200 g/7 oz white chocolate chips

1   Preheat the oven to 200°C/400°F/gas 6/fan oven 180°C. Grease and flour 12 muffin tin sections or line with paper liners.

2   Sift the dry ingredients into a large bowl and stir well.

3   Melt the butter either in a small bowl in the microwave or in a small saucepan. In a medium-sized bowl, beat together the milk, eggs and vanilla with a fork.

4   Add the egg mixture and the melted butter to the dry ingredients and fold together with a large metal spoon until just combined.

5   Gently fold in the blackberries and the white chocolate chips with a large metal spoon.

6   Divide the batter between the sections of the prepared muffin tin.

7   Bake for about 20–22 minutes until well risen and golden. And the muffins spring back when lightly pressed. If you added the berries to the batter frozen, you may need a couple more minutes' baking time.

8   Transfer to a wire rack to cool a little before eating.

Blueberry and buttermilk

So simple and yet so scrumptious, these muffins are best served warm, halved and spread with a little butter. Blueberry and buttermilk muffins are perfect for breakfast as they are a little less sweet than most muffins, very fruity and they have a slightly firmer crumb, which means that they don't disintegrate when you spread them with butter!

MAKES 11 MUFFINS

FOR THE BATTER
300 g/10½ oz plain (all-purpose) flour
2 tsp baking powder

⅛ tsp salt
170 g/6 oz caster (superfine) sugar
Grated zest of 1 lemon
250 g/8½ oz buttermilk
2 eggs

100 g/3½ oz butter
FOR THE FILLING
250 g/8½ oz fresh blueberries

1   Preheat the oven to 180°C/350°F/gas 4/fan oven 160°C. Grease and flour 11 muffin tin sections or line with paper liners.

2   Sift the flour, baking powder, salt and caster sugar into a large bowl. Stir in the lemon zest.

3   Combine the buttermilk and eggs in a small bowl, then beat well with a fork.

4   Melt the butter either in a small bowl in the microwave or in a small saucepan.

5   Add the egg mixture and the melted butter to the dry ingredients and gently fold together with a large metal spoon until just mixed.

6   Fold in the fresh blueberries, being careful not to over-mix.

7   Divide the batter evenly between the sections of the prepared muffin tin.

8   Bake for 23–25 minutes until well risen and golden and the muffins spring back when lightly pressed.

9   Transfer to a wire rack to cool a little before eating.

Christmas clementine and clove

This is a mouth-watering, not-too-sweet Christmas muffin. But you don't have to wait until Christmas; you can enjoy them any time of year. They are full of flavour and smell wonderful too! They are surprisingly good with cheese as the sweet and savoury flavours complement each other really well.

MAKES 10 MUFFINS

FOR THE BATTER
200 g/7 oz plain (all-purpose) flour
100 g/3½ oz wholemeal bread flour
1 tbsp baking powder

⅛ tsp salt
½ tsp ground cloves
40 g/1½ oz ground almonds
Grated zest and juice of three clementines
A little milk
2 eggs

1 tsp almond essence (extract)
100 g/3½ oz butter
170 g/6 oz dark muscovado sugar
FOR THE TOPPING
40 g/1½ oz demerara sugar
Gold dusting powder (optional)

1 Preheat the oven to 200°C/400°F/gas 6/fan oven 180°C. Grease and flour 10 muffin tin sections or line with paper liners.

2 Sift the flours, baking powder, salt and cloves into a bowl. Tip in all the little bits from the wholemeal flour that stayed in the sieve (strainer). Stir in the ground almonds and the clementine zest.

3 Make up the clementine juice to 170 g/6 oz with milk. Combine with the eggs and almond essence in a medium-sized bowl and mix thoroughly with a fork.

4 Melt the butter in a bowl in the microwave or in a small saucepan. Add the dark muscovado sugar to the melted butter and stir thoroughly.

5 Add the wet ingredients to the dry and fold together with a large metal spoon until just moistened.

6 Spoon into the prepared muffin tin and sprinkle evenly with demerara sugar.

7 Bake for 20–22 minutes, until the muffins are well risen and golden. The tops will spring back when gently pressed.

8 Transfer to a wire rack. Decorate the tops with gold dusting powder if you wish and serve warm.

Christmas in july

I'm not sure where the expression 'Christmas in July' comes from but it certainly applies to these muffins. Cranberries in anything makes you think of Christmas, especially combined with orange, but the addition of the rhubarb gives a fresh, light summery muffin. Perfect – Christmas in the middle of summer!

MAKES 14 MUFFINS

FOR THE BATTER
Grated zest and juice of 2 oranges
75 g/3 oz dried cranberries
310 g/11 oz plain (all-purpose) flour

185 g/6½ oz caster (superfine) sugar
1 tbsp baking powder
⅛ tsp salt
A little milk
190 g/6¾ oz double (heavy) cream
2 eggs

100 g/3½ oz butter
FOR THE FILLING
200 g/7 oz rhubarb, chopped into
   5 mm/¼ in dice

1   Put the orange zest in a large bowl.

2   Place your cranberries in a small bowl and pour over the juice from the two oranges. Leave to soak for an hour.

3   Preheat the oven to 180°C/350°F/gas 4/fan oven 160°C. Grease and flour 14 muffin tin sections or line with paper liners.

4   Sift the dry ingredients into the large bowl with the orange zest and mix well.

5   Drain the cranberries, saving the orange juice. Give the cranberries a slight press to get most of the juice out – but don't squeeze them dry. Weigh the reserved orange juice and make it up to 100 g/3½ oz with milk. Combine the orange juice and milk with the cream and the eggs but try not to thicken the cream as you mix it all together with a fork.

6   Melt the butter in a small bowl in the microwave or in a small saucepan.

7   Add all the wet ingredients to the dry ingredients and gently fold together with a large metal spoon until just moistened.

8   Gently fold in the chopped rhubarb and the soaked cranberries.

9   Spoon the batter into the prepared muffin tin sections.

10   Bake for about 23–25 minutes until well risen, and the tops spring back when gently pressed.

11   Transfer to a wire rack to cool a little before eating.

Cinnamon sugar, banana and raisin

These may look plain, but just break one open and smell that fabulous spicy aroma. The butter in the cinnamon topping gives it just a little more crunch than a dry topping, as well as a nice buttery flavour. You may find you need to use a small-bladed knife to help lever the muffins out of the tin without disturbing the topping.

MAKES 7 MUFFINS

FOR THE BATTER
60 g/2 oz butter
100 g/3¹/₂ oz light muscovado sugar
250 g/8¹/₂ oz very ripe bananas (unpeeled weight)

1 egg
140 g/4³/₄ oz plain (all-purpose) flour
20 g/³/₄ oz wholemeal bread flour
¹/₂ tsp salt
¹/₂ tsp bicarbonate of soda (baking soda)
¹/₂ tbsp ground cinnamon
35 g/1¹/₄ oz very hot water

FOR THE FILLING
70 g/2¹/₂ oz raisins
FOR THE TOPPING
1 tsp ground cinnamon
60 g/2 oz granulated sugar
10 g melted butter

1 Preheat the oven to 180°C/350°F/gas 4/fan oven 160°C. Grease and flour seven muffin tin sections or line with paper liners.

2 Melt the butter in a large bowl over a pan of simmering water or briefly in the microwave. Place the bowl on your work surface and add the sugar. Mix thoroughly.

3 Peel the bananas and mash them in a medium-sized bowl with a fork. Add them to the butter and sugar and mix thoroughly.

4 In the same bowl you used for the bananas, beat the egg with the fork. Add to the butter mixture and mix well.

5 Sift the flours, salt, bicarbonate of soda and the ground cinnamon into a medium-sized bowl. Add back in all the little bits that sieved out of the wholemeal flour.

6 Add the half the flour mixture to the butter mixture and mix together well. Add the hot water and mix it in thoroughly. Finally mix in the remaining flour.

7 Stir in the raisins.

8 Spoon the batter into the prepared muffin tin sections.

9 Combine the topping ingredients in a small bowl. Sprinkle the topping evenly over the muffins.

10 Bake for 30–33 minutes until the muffins are well risen and spring back when you gently press the tops.

11 Transfer to a wire rack to cool a little before eating.

Fresh orange and almond

These muffins are deliciously sweet and fruity, wonderfully moist and even have a delightful stickiness about them! The freshness and piquancy of the oranges creates a delicious contrast to the almonds, which I use quite a lot in my cooking as they impart such a wonderful texture and flavour.

MAKES 14 MUFFINS

FOR THE BATTER
310 g/11 oz plain (all-purpose) flour
170 g/6 oz caster (superfine) sugar

1 tbsp baking powder
1/8 tsp salt
60 g/2 oz ground almonds
8 medium-sized oranges
A little milk

2 eggs
1/2 tsp almond essence (extract)
100 g/3 1/2 oz butter
FOR THE TOPPING
40 g/1 1/2 oz demerara sugar

1 Preheat the oven to 200°C/400°F/gas 6/fan oven 180°C. Grease and flour 14 muffin tin sections or line with paper liners.

2 Sift the flour, sugar, baking powder and salt into a large bowl. Stir in the ground almonds.

3 Squeeze the juice from two of the oranges. Make up the juice to 170 g/6 oz with milk and set aside. Grate the zest from five of the oranges and add the zest to the flour mixture, stirring well.

4 Now prepare all the unsqueezed oranges as described on page 16. Cut a slice off the top and bottom of each one. Place the cut bottom of the orange down on the chopping board. Starting at the top of the orange and carefully following the curve of the fruit, cut away a portion of the skin, taking off all the white pith. Continue to do this all the way around the orange, then pick it up and carefully, with your knife, remove each section of orange from between the membranes.

5 Weigh out 200 g/7 oz of the flesh for the filling, then chop into small pieces. Reserve 14 of the remaining sections for the topping.

6 Place the orange juice and milk, eggs and almond essence in a medium-sized bowl. Mix the ingredients thoroughly with a fork. Melt the butter in a small bowl in the microwave or in a saucepan.

7 Add all the wet ingredients to the dry, and fold together with a large metal spoon until just moistened.

8 Very gently fold in the pieces of orange for the filling.

9 Spoon into the prepared muffin tin sections.

10 Cut each orange segment for the topping into three pieces and place on top of each muffin. Sprinkle the demerara sugar evenly over the tops.

11 Bake for 24–27 minutes, until the muffins are well risen and golden. The tops will spring back when gently pressed.

12 Transfer to a wire rack to cool a little before eating.

Lemon and almond

This flavour of this muffin is clean and fresh, with a nice, crisp crunch from the flaked almonds on top. The lemon gives them just a subtle touch of sharpness, which is quite unusual and delicious. As you know, I do like muffins warm, but these muffins are also particularly good cold.

MAKES 10 MUFFINS

FOR THE BATTER
235 g/8¼ oz plain (all-purpose) flour
170 g/6 oz caster (superfine) sugar
1 tbsp baking powder
⅛ tsp salt
100 g/3½ oz ground almonds
Grated zest and juice of 2 lemons
A little milk

2 eggs
1 tsp almond essence (extract)
100 g/3½ oz butter
FOR THE TOPPING
50 g/1¾ oz flaked (slivered) almonds

1. Preheat the oven to 200°C/400°F/gas 6/fan oven 180°C. Grease and flour 10 muffin tin sections or line with paper liners.

2. Sift the flour, caster sugar, baking powder and salt into a large bowl. Stir in the ground almonds and the lemon zest.

3. Make the lemon juice up to 170 g/6 oz with milk. Combine with the eggs and almond essence in a medium-sized bowl and mix thoroughly with a fork.

4. Melt the butter in a small bowl in the microwave or in a small saucepan.

5. Add the wet ingredients to the dry and fold together with a large metal spoon until just moistened.

6. Spoon the batter into the prepared muffin tin sections and sprinkle evenly with the flaked almonds.

7. Bake for 20–23 minutes, until the muffins are well risen and golden and the tops spring back when lightly pressed.

8. Transfer to a wire rack to cool a little before eating.

Molasses sugar, apple and raisin

You might expect these to be spicy, like gingerbread, because of the rich colour and texture. But they are a surprisingly light, very fruity muffin with the lingering, full flavour of molasses. Don't bother to peel the apples when you prepare them – just core them, then chop the flesh, including the peel.

MAKES 12 MUFFINS

FOR THE BATTER
300 g/10½ oz plain (all-purpose) flour
1 tbsp baking powder
⅛ tsp salt
185 g/6½ oz milk

2 eggs
100 g/3½ oz butter
185 g/6½ oz molasses sugar
25 g/1 oz molasses
FOR THE FILLING
250 g/8½ oz finely chopped unpeeled
   eating (dessert) apple

100 g/3½ oz raisins
FOR THE TOPPING
12 wafer-thin slices of apple
40 g/1½ oz demerara sugar

1　Preheat the oven to 180°C/350°F/gas 4/fan oven 160°C. Grease and flour 12 muffin tin sections or line with paper liners.

2　Sift the flour, baking powder and salt into a large bowl. Combine the milk and eggs in a medium-sized bowl and beat together with a fork.

3　Melt the butter in a medium-sized bowl in the microwave or in a small saucepan. Stir the molasses sugar and the molasses into the melted butter with a fork until most of the sugar has dissolved. You may still have a few small lumps.

4　Add the egg mixture and the butter mixture to the dry ingredients and fold together with a large metal spoon until just combined.

5　Fold the filling into the muffin batter, being careful not to over-mix. Spoon the batter into the prepared muffin tin sections. Top each muffin with a slice of apple and sprinkle with the demerara sugar.

6　Bake for about 25–30 minutes until well risen and golden and the tops spring back when gently pressed.

7　Transfer to a wire rack to cool a little before eating.

New year after shock

After Shock is a bright-red, hot-tasting, cinnamon liqueur that you can buy in most large supermarkets. So, in essence this is a cinnamon and raisin muffin, but with a serious kick! I thought it would be an interesting way to start a new year – something familiar but with a fresh new twist. This muffin is equally good served hot or cold.

MAKES 12 MUFFINS

FOR THE FILLING
200 g/7 oz raisins
30 g/2 tbsp After Shock liqueur

FOR THE BATTER
310 g/11 oz plain (all-purpose) flour
170 g/6 oz light muscovado sugar
1 tbsp baking powder
⅛ tsp salt
100 g/3½ oz butter

190 g/6¾ oz double (heavy) cream
100 g/3½ oz After Shock liqueur
2 eggs

FOR THE TOPPING
40 g/1½ oz demerara sugar

1   Preheat the oven to 180°C/350°F/gas 4/fan oven 160°C. Grease and flour 12 muffin tin sections or line with paper liners. Put the raisins in a bowl with the After Shock and leave to soak for at least one hour.

2   Sift the dry batter ingredients into a large bowl and stir well. You will need to push the muscovado sugar through the sieve (strainer) with the back of a spoon.

3   Melt the butter in a small bowl in the microwave or in a small saucepan. Combine the double cream, After Shock liqueur and eggs in a medium-sized bowl and mix together well with a fork. Try not to thicken the cream.

4   Add the egg mixture and the melted butter to the dry ingredients and fold together with a large metal spoon until just moistened.

5   Fold in the raisins and any unabsorbed After Shock liqueur. Spoon the batter into the prepared muffin tin sections.

6   Top the muffins with the demerara sugar.

7   Bake for about 22–24 minutes until well risen and golden and the tops of the muffins spring back when lightly pressed.

8   Transfer to a wire rack to cool a little before eating.

Raspberries and cream

Oh, look at that picture! Just as you might expect from the photograph and the name, these muffins are rich and sweet with a cake-like texture, beautifully dotted with luscious, red raspberries. You can use fresh fruit in season, or you can make the muffins with frozen raspberries if you fancy a touch of English summer when it's cold outside.

MAKES 12 MUFFINS

FOR THE BATTER
310 g/11 oz plain (all-purpose) flour
185 g/6½ oz caster (superfine) sugar

1 tbsp baking powder
⅛ tsp salt
100 g/3½ oz butter
2 eggs
100 g/3½ oz milk

190 g/6¾ oz double (heavy) cream
FOR THE FILLING
250 g/8½ oz fresh or frozen raspberries

1 Preheat the oven to 180°C/350°F/gas 4/fan oven 160°C. Grease and flour 12 muffin tin sections or line with paper liners.

2 Sift all the dry ingredients into a large bowl and mix well.

3 Melt the butter in a small bowl in the microwave or in a small saucepan. Combine the eggs, milk and cream in a medium-sized bowl. Mix together with a fork but try not to thicken the cream.

4 Add the wet ingredients to the dry ingredients and fold together with a large metal spoon until just moistened.

5 Gently fold in the raspberries and spoon the batter into the prepared muffin tin sections.

6 Bake for about 23–25 minutes until well risen and golden and the tops spring back when gently pressed.

7 Transfer to a wire rack to cool a little before eating.

Red grapes, vanilla sugar and aniseed

This is a sweet, juicy muffin delicately spiced with vanilla and aniseed. Beware – the grapes get incredibly hot while the muffins are baking, so give them a good 20 minutes to cool down to room temperature before you eat them. If you wash the grapes, dry them very thoroughly on kitchen paper before adding to the mixture or they will make it too wet.

MAKES 13 MUFFINS

FOR THE BATTER
8 g/1 tbsp whole aniseed
300 g/10¹/₂ oz plain (all-purpose) flour
185 g/6¹/₂ oz vanilla sugar (see page 10)
1 tbsp baking powder

¹/₈ tsp salt
2 eggs
185 g/6¹/₂ oz milk
100 g/3¹/₂ oz butter
FOR THE FILLING
250 g/8¹/₂ oz red grapes, halved

FOR THE TOPPING
About 100 g/3¹/₂ oz red grapes, sliced
40 g/1¹/₂ oz demerara sugar
10 g/scant ¹/₂ oz vanilla sugar
About 20 white sugar cubes, lightly crushed

1. Preheat the oven to 200°C/400°F/gas 6/fan oven 180°C. Grease and flour 13 muffin tin sections or line with paper liners. Grind the aniseed in a spice grinder or clean coffee mill.

2. Sift all the dry ingredients into a large bowl; tip in any aniseed that remained in the sieve (strainer).

3. Combine the eggs and milk in a medium-sized bowl. Melt the butter in a small bowl in the microwave or in a small saucepan.

4. Add the egg mixture and the melted butter to the dry ingredients and gently fold together with a large metal spoon until just moistened. Fold in the halved grapes.

5. Spoon the batter into the prepared muffin tin sections. Place three pieces of grape on top of each muffin. Combine the demerara and vanilla sugar in a small bowl, then sprinkle the mixed sugars evenly over the muffins.

6   Crush the sugar cubes, a few at a time, in a mortar and pestle or in a bowl with the end of a rolling pin. Do this lightly, leaving them in fairly large chunks or they will disintegrate while the muffins are baking. Scatter these over the muffins.

7   Bake for about 23–25 minutes until well risen and golden and the tops spring back when gently pressed.

8   Transfer to a wire rack to cool for at least 20 minutes before serving.

Rhubarb and custard

These flavours are such a classic and they work beautifully in this muffin. The custard recipe is quite easy and the taste is wonderful, but if you do use a tub of fresh ready-made custard, add a teaspoon of vanilla essence to the 210 g/7½ oz of custard you need for the recipe. If you want to make the custard to serve separately, leave out the extra vanilla at the end.

MAKES 12 MUFFINS

FOR THE CUSTARD
3 egg yolks
60 g/2 oz vanilla sugar (see page 10)
1 tsp cornflour (cornstarch)
285 g/10 oz whole or semi-skimmed milk

1 tsp vanilla essence (extract)
FOR THE BATTER
300 g/10½ oz plain (all-purpose) flour
1 tbsp baking powder
⅛ tsp salt
100 g/3½ oz caster (superfine) sugar
80 g/3 oz vanilla sugar

2 eggs
100 g/3½ oz butter
FOR THE FILLING
250 g/8½ oz rhubarb, chopped into
   5 mm/¼ in dice
FOR THE TOPPING
Icing sugar for dusting

1 Preheat the oven to 180°C/350°F/gas 4/fan oven 160°C. Grease and flour 12 muffin tin sections or line with paper liners.

2 Make the custard. Place the egg yolks, sugar and cornflour in a medium-sized bowl, then whisk the ingredients until thoroughly mixed.

3 Place the milk in a medium saucepan and heat over a medium heat, stirring from time to time with a rubber spatula or wooden spoon for about 5 minutes until the milk is almost ready to boil.

4 Take the pan off the heat. With the whisk in one hand and the pan of warm milk in the other, slowly pour the milk on to the egg mixture, whisking vigorously all the time until all the milk has been added.

5 Now return the milk and egg mixture to the saucepan, place the pan back on the medium heat and give it another good whisk. Stir the custard slowly all the time for about 5 minutes until it thickens. The custard should be thick enough to coat the back of the spoon.

6 Remove from the heat, and add the teaspoon of vanilla. Pour the custard back into the bowl and set aside to cool, stirring from time to time.

7 Sift the dry batter ingredients into a large bowl and stir well.

8 Lightly beat the eggs in a small bowl.

9 Add 210 g/7½ oz of the custard, the melted butter and the beaten eggs to the dry ingredients and gently fold together with a large metal spoon until just moistened.

10 Gently fold in the chopped rhubarb. Spoon the batter into the prepared muffin tin sections.

11 Bake for about 23–25 minutes until well risen and golden and the tops spring back when gently pressed.

12 Transfer to a wire rack and dust heavily with icing sugar.

Rhubarb, apple and sultana custard

I have revisited an old favourite flavour combination from my book Mad about Bread *in this muffin recipe. I had some rhubarb left over from another recipe and didn't want to waste it, so I remembered the pie I cobbled together with custard, which turned into Rhubarb, Apple and Sultana Choppy Loaf – and which has now become this lovely muffin!*

MAKES 13 MUFFINS

FOR THE CUSTARD
285 g/10 oz whole or semi-skimmed milk
1 tsp vanilla essence (extract)
3 egg yolks
1 tsp cornflour (cornstarch)
60 g/2 oz vanilla sugar

FOR THE BATTER
300 g/10½ oz plain (all-purpose) flour
1 tbsp baking powder
⅛ tsp salt
100 g/3½ oz caster (superfine) sugar
80 g/3 oz vanilla sugar (see page 10)
100 g/3½ oz butter
2 eggs

FOR THE FILLING
100 g/3½ oz rhubarb, chopped into
    5 mm/¼ in dice
140 g/4¾ oz finely chopped unpeeled
    eating (dessert) apple
70 g/2½ oz sultanas (golden raisins)
FOR THE TOPPING
40 g/1½ oz demerara sugar

1   Preheat the oven to 180°C/350°F/gas 4/fan oven 160°C. Grease and flour 13 sections of muffin tin or line with paper liners.

2   Make the custard. Place the egg yolks, sugar and cornflour in a medium-sized bowl then, using a whisk, combine the ingredients until thoroughly mixed. Place the milk in a medium saucepan and heat over a medium heat, stirring from time to time with a rubber spatula or wooden spoon until the milk is almost ready to boil – it will take about 5 minutes and you will see the first few bubbles come up.

3   Take the pan off the heat. With the whisk in one hand and the pan of warm milk in the other, slowly pour the milk on to the egg mixture, whisking vigorously all the time until all the milk has been added to the eggs.

4   Now return the milk and egg mixture to the saucepan, place the pan back on the medium heat and give it another good whisk. Stir the custard slowly all the time with your wooden spoon or spatula until it thickens – this will take about 5 minutes and it usually finishes just as the sauce tries to come up to the boil – again, you may see the odd bubble trying to break the surface. The custard should be thick enough to coat the back of the spoon.

5   Remove from the heat, and add the teaspoon of vanilla. Pour the custard back into the bowl and set aside to cool. Give it a stir from time to time while you mix up the batter to help it cool.

6   Sift the dry batter ingredients into a large bowl and stir well.

7   Melt the butter in a small bowl in the microwave or in a small saucepan. Lightly beat the eggs in a small bowl.

8   Add 210 g/7½ oz of the custard, the melted butter and the eggs to the dry ingredients and gently fold together with a large metal spoon until just moistened. (If you have used shop-bought custard, add 1 tsp of vanilla as you mix it into the dry ingredients.)

8   Fold in the rhubarb, apple and sultanas. Spoon the batter into the prepared muffin tin sections. Share around the demerara sugar for the topping.

10   Bake for about 23–25 minutes until well risen and golden and the tops spring back when gently pressed.

11   Transfer to a wire rack to cool a little before eating.

Rhubarb, ginger and pistachio

These muffins look and taste fabulous, with their beautiful rainbow colours and unusual, but delicious, flavour combination. Under that crisp sugary top, you've got tart pink rhubarb, spiky preserved ginger and buttery, bright green pistachio nuts, all tumbled together in a soft, spicy muffin. Fabulous!

MAKES 11 MUFFINS

FOR THE BATTER

300 g/10¹/₂ oz plain (all-purpose) flour

¹/₂ tsp bicarbonate of soda (baking soda)

1 tsp baking powder

¹/₄ tsp salt

¹/₂ tsp ground ginger

¹/₂ tsp cinnamon

185 g/6¹/₂ oz light muscovado sugar

2 eggs

70 g/2¹/₂ oz plain yoghurt

70 g/2¹/₂ oz milk

1 tsp vanilla essence (extract)

70 g/2¹/₂ oz butter

FOR THE FILLING

200 g/7 oz rhubarb, chopped into 5 mm/¹/₄ in dice

40 g/1¹/₂ oz pistachio nuts, lightly chopped

1 ball of preserved stem ginger, finely chopped

FOR THE TOPPING

30 g/1 oz demerara sugar

1 Preheat the oven to 200°C/400°F/gas 6/fan oven 180°C. Grease and flour 11 muffin tin sections or line with paper liners.

2 In a large bowl, sift together the plain flour, bicarbonate of soda, baking powder, salt, ground ginger, cinnamon and light muscovado sugar. Stir well.

3 Place the eggs, yoghurt, milk and vanilla into a medium-sized bowl and beat together with a fork.

4 Melt the butter in a small bowl in the microwave or in a small saucepan.

5 Combine the prepared rhubarb, pistachio nuts and stem ginger in a bowl and set aside.

6 Add the egg mixture and the melted butter to the dry ingredients and fold together with a large metal spoon until just combined. Gently fold in the rhubarb, pistachio nuts and stem ginger.

7 Spoon the batter into the prepared muffin tin sections. Sprinkle the topping evenly over the muffins.

8 Bake for 20–25 minutes until well risen and golden and the tops spring back when gently pressed.

9 Transfer to a wire rack to cool before eating.

Strawberry and rhubarb

These muffins are based on one of my family's favourite pies! They are full of fruit and very moist, with the lovely green and pink rhubarb complemented by the red strawberries and golden muffin crumb. I like to use muscovado sugar and just a hint of ginger to round out the flavour, too.

MAKES 12 MUFFINS

FOR THE BATTER
300 g/10½ oz plain (all-purpose) flour
1 tbsp baking powder
¼ tsp salt
¼ tsp ground ginger
185 g/6½ oz light muscovado sugar
100 g/3½ oz butter
2 eggs
185 g/6½ oz milk
1 tsp vanilla essence (extract)

FOR THE FILLING
30 g/1 oz sultanas (golden raisins)
100 g/3½ oz rhubarb, chopped into 5 mm/¼ in dice
200 g/7 oz strawberries, chopped

FOR THE TOPPING
40 g/1½ oz demerara sugar

1 Preheat the oven to 200°C/400°F/gas 6/fan oven 180°C. Grease and flour 12 muffin tin sections or line with paper liners.

2 Sift the dry batter ingredients into a large bowl, pushing the sugar through the sieve (strainer) with the back of a spoon.

3 Melt the butter in a small bowl in the microwave or in a small saucepan.

4 Combine the eggs, milk and vanilla in a medium-sized bowl.

5 Add the egg mixture and the melted butter to the dry ingredients and fold together with a large metal spoon until just combined.

6 Combine the filling ingredients in a bowl, and then gently fold into the batter. Be careful not to over-stir the batter.

7 Spoon the batter into the prepared muffin tin sections and sprinkle evenly with sugar.

8 Bake for 25–27 minutes until well risen and golden and the muffins spring back when lightly pressed.

9 Transfer to a wire rack to cool a little before eating.

Strawberry, almond and orange

Citrus fruit really brings out the flavour in strawberries. Here I've combined strawberries with fresh orange and Grand Marnier liqueur to lift the flavour of the strawberries and scent the muffin mixture. Ground almonds also help to provide a moist texture and there is a scattering of flaked almonds on top to give a nice crunch!

MAKES 15 MUFFINS

FOR THE BATTER
310 g/11 oz plain (all-purpose) flour
170 g/6 oz caster (superfine) sugar
1 tbsp baking powder
1/8 tsp salt

50 g/1³/₄ oz ground almonds
Grated zest and juice of 1 orange
100 g/3¹/₂ oz butter
A little milk
100 g/3¹/₂ oz Grand Marnier
1 tsp almond essence (extract)
2 eggs

FOR THE FILLING
400 g/14 oz strawberries, chopped into small pieces
FOR THE TOPPING
50 g/1³/₄ oz flaked (slivered) almonds

1. Preheat the oven to 200°C/400°F/gas 6/fan oven 180°C. Grease and flour 15 muffin tin sections or line with paper liners.

2. Sift the flour, caster sugar, baking powder and salt into a large bowl. Stir in the ground almonds and the orange zest.

3. Melt the butter in a small bowl in the microwave or in a small saucepan.

4. Make the orange juice up to 100 g/3¹/₂ oz with milk. Combine with the Grand Marnier, almond essence and eggs in a medium-sized bowl. Mix well with a fork.

5. Add the wet ingredients to the dry and fold together with a large metal spoon until just moistened.

6. Very gently fold in the strawberries.

7. Spoon the batter into the prepared muffin tin sections.

8. Sprinkle evenly with the flaked almonds.

9. Bake for 22–25 minutes, until the muffins are well risen and golden and the tops spring back when gently pressed.

10. Transfer to a wire rack to cool before eating.

Strawberry, pecan and coconut

The puréed strawberries give these muffins a beautiful, pale pink colour. Tucked inside are toasted pecans, sweet coconut and even more strawberries! The inspiration behind these muffins came from a description of a cake my mum made long ago that had similar ingredients, except that she used a packet of flavoured red gelatine to give the cake a pink colour.

MAKES 12 MUFFINS

FOR THE BATTER
200 g/7 oz strawberries, puréed
Grated zest and juice of 1 lemon
310 g/11 oz plain (all-purpose) flour

170 g/6 oz caster (superfine) sugar
1 tbsp baking powder
1/8 tsp salt
50 g/1³/₄ oz sweetened desiccated (shredded) coconut
100 g/3¹/₂ oz oil

2 eggs
FOR THE FILLING
50 g/1³/₄ oz pecans, toasted (see page 10) and roughly chopped
150 g/5 oz strawberries, chopped into small pieces

1　Preheat the oven to 200°C/400°F/gas 6/fan oven 180°C. Grease and flour 12 muffin tin sections or line with paper liners. Whiz the strawberries and 1 tablespoon of lemon juice in a blender or food processor. Use a rubber spatula to get as much of the purée out of the blender as possible and place in a medium-sized bowl.

2　Put the lemon zest into a large bowl and sift the flour, sugar, baking powder and salt into the same bowl. Stir well and then stir in the coconut.

3　Combine the oil and eggs with the puréed strawberries and beat well with a fork.

4　Add the wet ingredients to the dry and fold together with a large metal spoon until just moistened.

5　Gently fold in the toasted pecans and the chopped strawberries.

6　Spoon the batter into the prepared muffin tin sections.

7　Bake for 20–22 minutes, until the muffins are well risen and the tops spring back when pressed.

8　Transfer to a wire rack to cool a bit before eating.

NUT AND ALCOHOL MUFFINS

In this section I've used many different varieties of nuts, as well as some seeds and grains, to add wonderful taste, texture and visual appeal to your muffins. The nuts can be used whole, chopped, flaked or shredded, and if you toast them first this will bring out a much deeper flavour and make them extra crisp. Ground nuts are great for adding moisture to a muffin, too – and you don't have to stick to ground almonds, try ground peanuts, cashew nuts and macadamias.

I love the concentrated, intense kick and heady aroma that alcohol brings to baking. Dried fruits soaked in alcohol work beautifully but even if you just add the alcohol to the batter, the sweet, concentrated intensity of both the alcohol and the dried fruit really complement each other well. That's not to say that alcohol doesn't work with fresh fruit in a muffin too – just think cocktail!

Almond, blackberry and coconut

I really like these muffins. They came about one day when we had collected some fat blackberries while we were out for a walk. I was going to make a simple muffin mix with them, but then I looked in the cupboard and saw bits and pieces that needed using up, and that's how this combination came together.

MAKES 12 MUFFINS

FOR THE BATTER
320 g/11¼ oz plain (all-purpose) flour
1 tbsp baking powder
⅛ tsp salt

170 g/6 oz caster (superfine) sugar
60 g/2 oz ground almonds
20 g/¾ oz sweetened desiccated
  (shredded) coconut
½ tsp almond essence (extract)
100 g/3½ oz oil
200 g/7 oz milk

2 eggs
FOR THE FILLING
170 g/6 oz blackberries
FOR THE TOPPING
40 g/1½ oz flaked (slivered) almonds
40 g/1½ oz sweetened shredded coconut

1 Preheat the oven to 180°C/350°C/gas 4/fan oven 160°C. Grease and flour 12 muffin tin sections or line with paper liners.

2 Sift all the flour, baking powder, salt and sugar into a large bowl. Add the ground almonds and coconut and mix thoroughly.

3 Combine the wet ingredients in a medium-sized bowl and beat thoroughly with a fork.

4 Add the wet ingredients to the dry and fold together with a large metal spoon until just combined. Fold in the blackberries.

5 Divide the batter evenly between the sections of the muffin tin.

6 Sprinkle the flaked almonds, then the coconut evenly over the muffins.

7 Bake for 25–28 minutes until golden and well risen and the muffins spring back when lightly pressed.

8 Transfer to a wire rack to cool a little before eating.

Christmas cranberry, grand marnier and almond

Imagine this: the heady scent of Grand Marnier, the delicate crunch of almonds and demerara sugar, the jewel-like red cranberries bursting in your mouth and the melting, white chocolate! For extra luxury, I dust the tops of the baked muffins with gold cake-decorating powder. Fabulous for Christmas — but just as good at any time!

MAKES 12 MUFFINS

FOR THE BATTER
310 g/11 oz plain (all-purpose) flour
170 g/6 oz caster (superfine) sugar
1 tbsp baking powder
⅛ tsp salt

50 g/1¾ oz ground almonds
100 g/3½ oz Grand Marnier
100 g/3½ oz milk
100 g/3½ oz oil
1 tsp almond essence (extract)
2 eggs

FOR THE FILLING
200 g/7 oz fresh or frozen cranberries
150 g/5 oz white chocolate, chopped
FOR THE TOPPING
40 g/1½ oz flaked (slivered) almonds
30 g/1 oz demerara sugar
Gold dusting powder (optional)

1 Preheat the oven to 200°C/400°F/gas 6/fan oven 180°C. Grease and flour 12 muffin tin sections or line with paper liners.

2 Sift the flour, sugar, baking powder and salt into a large bowl. Stir in the ground almonds.

3 Combine the wet ingredients in a medium-sized bowl and mix thoroughly with a fork.

4 Add the wet ingredients to the dry and fold together with a large metal spoon until just moistened. Very gently fold in the cranberries and chocolate.

5 Spoon into the prepared muffin tin sections and sprinkle evenly with the flaked almonds and demerara sugar.

6 Bake for 22–25 minutes until the muffins are well risen and golden and the tops spring back when gently pressed.

7 Transfer to a wire rack. Decorate the almond topping with gold dusting powder if you wish and serve warm.

Crème de cacao

If you've no chocolate in the house, you probably have some cocoa in the cupboard and if you have some crème de cacao liqueur, then you're away! This recipe makes a rich, chocolatey muffin, very good on its own but one that also enjoys being dressed up – possibly with ice cream and chocolate sauce or maybe with a huge dollop of softly whipped double cream!

MAKES 12 MUFFINS

FOR THE BATTER
260 g/9 oz plain (all-purpose) flour
50 g/1³/₄ oz cocoa (unsweetened chocolate) powder
1 tbsp baking powder
¹/₈ tsp salt
170 g/6 oz light muscovado sugar
2 eggs
200 g/7 oz crème de cacao
100 g/3¹/₂ oz double (heavy) cream
1 tsp vanilla essence (extract)
100 g/3¹/₂ oz butter
FOR DUSTING
Cocoa powder and icing (confectioners') sugar

1 Preheat the oven to 180°C/350°F/gas 4/fan oven 160°C. Grease and flour 12 muffin tin sections or line with paper liners.

2 Sift the dry ingredients into a large bowl, using the back of a spoon to push the light muscovado sugar through the sieve (strainer).

3 Combine the eggs, crème de cacao, double cream and vanilla in a medium-sized bowl and mix well with a fork. Try to avoid thickening the cream. Melt the butter in a small bowl in the microwave or in a small saucepan.

4 Add all the wet ingredients to the dry ingredients and gently fold together with a large metal spoon until just moistened.

5 Spoon the batter into the sections of a prepared muffin tin.

6 Bake for about 23–25 minutes until well risen and the tops of the muffins spring back when pressed.

7 Transfer to a wire rack to cool and little. Dust the tops of the muffins with cocoa powder and then icing sugar, while they are still warm.

Golden syrup and oatmeal

These muffins will never be as flashy as chocolate or fruity muffins, but they are sweet and deliciously sticky. You won't really see the blob of golden syrup in the centre of the muffin once it is cooked – but you will taste it! I think these are a really fantastic storecupboard-ingredient muffin that's sure to please.

MAKES 10 MUFFINS

FOR THE BATTER
285 g/10 oz plain (all-purpose) flour
125 g/4¼ oz light muscovado sugar
2 tsp baking powder
¼ tsp salt

50 g/1¾ oz porridge oats
170 g/6 oz milk
2 eggs
100 g/3½ oz butter
75 g/3 oz golden (light corn) syrup

FOR THE FILLING
Golden syrup
FOR THE TOPPING
20 g/¾ oz jumbo oats
20 g/¾ oz demerara sugar
FOR BRUSHING
60 g/2 oz golden syrup, warmed

1 Preheat the oven to 200°C/400°F/gas 6/fan oven 180°C. Grease and flour 10 muffin tin sections or line with paper liners.

2 Sift the flour, sugar, baking powder and salt into a large bowl, pushing the light muscovado sugar through the sieve (strainer) with the back of a spoon. Stir in the porridge oats.

3 Combine the milk and eggs in a medium-sized bowl and mix thoroughly with a fork.

4 Melt the butter in a small bowl in the microwave or in a small saucepan. Stir the measured golden syrup into the melted butter and mix well.

5 Add all the wet ingredients to the dry and fold the mixture together with a large metal spoon until just moistened.

6 Spoon in enough batter to half-fill each prepared muffin tin section. Place a scant half-teaspoon of golden syrup into the centre of each and then cover with the remaining batter. (If you buy golden syrup in a squeezy bottle, this is really quick and easy.)

7 Sprinkle the oats evenly over the muffins, then the sugar.

8 Bake for 20–22 minutes, until the muffins are well risen and golden and the tops spring back when gently pressed.

9 Transfer to a wire rack and brush with the warmed golden syrup. Allow to cool a little before eating.

Honey, tahini and sesame

The combination of honey, lemon and tahini paste in this batter produces a muffin with a wonderful smell and taste. The muffins are light in both texture and colour, and the sesame seeds and demerara sugar make a crunchy topping with a beautifully speckled appearance.

MAKES 11 MUFFINS

FOR THE BATTER
330 g/11½ oz plain (all-purpose) flour
135 g/4½ oz caster (superfine) sugar
2 tsp baking powder
¼ tsp salt

Grated zest and juice of 1 large lemon
A little milk
100 g/3½ oz oil
50 g/1¾ oz clear honey
25 g/1 oz tahini paste
2 eggs
15 g/½ oz sesame seeds

FOR THE FILLING
Clear honey
FOR THE TOPPING
30 g/1 oz demerara sugar
25 g/1 oz sesame seeds

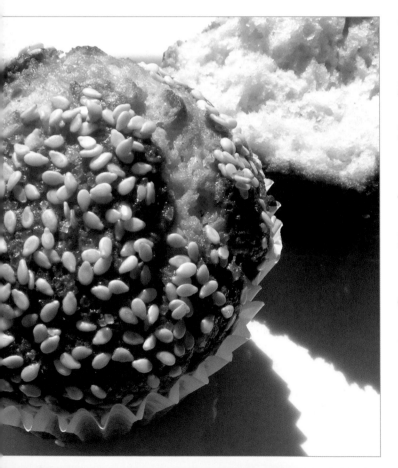

1 Preheat the oven to 200°C/400°F/gas 6/fan oven 180°C. Grease and flour 11 muffin tin sections or line with paper liners.

2 Sift the flour, sugar, baking powder and salt into a large bowl, then stir in the lemon zest.

3 Make the lemon juice up to 170 g/6 oz with milk and combine with the eggs and oil in a medium-sized bowl, mixing well with a fork.

4 Warm the measured honey and stir in the tahini paste with a fork.

5 Add all the wet ingredients to the dry. With a large metal spoon, fold the mixture together until just moistened.

6 Fold the sesame seeds into the batter and then half-fill each muffin section with batter.

7 Place a half-teaspoon of honey on top of the batter in each muffin section and then fill the sections with the rest of the batter.

8 Sprinkle the topping over evenly and bake for
   20–22 minutes, until the muffins are well risen
   and golden and the tops spring back when gently
   pressed.

9 Transfer to a wire rack to cool a little before
   serving.

Kahlua and cream

A deeply indulgent coffee liqueur and cream muffin, finished with an Irish coffee-style topping, you won't find this kind of unique recipe anywhere but in my recipe collection! It's a fabulous muffin to serve to friends, who are always impressed with the most imaginative recipes.

MAKES 12 MUFFINS

FOR THE BATTER
300 g/10½ oz plain (all-purpose) flour
1 tbsp baking powder
⅛ tsp salt

5 g/1 tbsp instant coffee powder or granules
170 g/6 oz light muscovado sugar
2 eggs
100 g/3½ oz Kahlua coffee liqueur
190 g/6¾ oz double (heavy) cream

1 tsp vanilla essence (extract)
100 g/3½ oz butter
FOR THE TOPPING
100 g/3½ oz double (heavy) cream
30 g/1 oz demerara sugar

1. Preheat the oven to 200°C/400°F/gas 6/fan oven 180°C. Grease and flour 12 muffin tin sections or line with paper liners.

2. Sift the dry ingredients into a large bowl, using a spoon to push the coffee and light muscovado sugar through the sieve (strainer).

3. Combine the eggs, Kahlua, double cream and vanilla in a medium-sized bowl and mix well with a fork. Try not to thicken the cream. Melt the butter in a small bowl in the microwave or in a small saucepan.

4. Add all the wet ingredients to the dry ingredients and gently fold together with a large metal spoon until just moistened.

5. Spoon the batter into the prepared muffin tin.

6. Spoon double cream over the muffins (about ½ tbsp each), then sprinkle with demerara sugar.

7. Bake for 20–23 minutes until well risen and golden and the tops of the spring back when gently pressed.

8. Transfer to a wire rack to cool a little before eating.

Macadamia, coconut and pineapple

The whole flavour experience of this tender muffin, with sweet coconut, juicy pineapple, buttery, crunchy macadamia nuts and a sensational shot of Malibu, is all very relaxed and easy going – just as you would expect from a muffin with so much laid-back Caribbean influence. Think of sun, sand and palm trees as you sit back and enjoy!

MAKES 12 MUFFINS

FOR THE BATTER
310 g/11 oz plain (all-purpose) flour
170 g/6 oz caster (superfine) sugar
1 tbsp baking powder
⅛ tsp salt

50 g/1¾ oz sweetened desiccated (shredded) coconut
100 g/3½ oz butter
170 g/6 oz pineapple juice from a can
A little milk
100 g/3½ oz Malibu
2 eggs

FOR THE FILLING
160 g/5½ oz canned pineapple pieces (drained weight), finely chopped
100 g/3½ oz macadamia nuts, toasted (see page 10) and roughly chopped

FOR THE TOPPING
50 g/1¾ oz sweetened desiccated coconut

1. Preheat the oven to 200°C/400°F/gas 6/fan oven 180°C. Grease and flour 12 muffin tin sections or line with paper liners.

2. Sift the flour, sugar, baking powder and salt into a large bowl, then stir in the coconut.

3. Melt the butter in a small bowl in the microwave or in a small saucepan. Make up the pineapple juice to 170 g/6 oz with milk. Combine this mixture in a medium-sized bowl with the Malibu and eggs and beat well with a fork.

4. Add the wet ingredients to the dry, and fold together with a large metal spoon until just moistened.

5. Fold the pineapple pieces gently into the batter mixture with the macadamia nuts.

6. Spoon the batter into the prepared muffin tin sections.

7. Sprinkle the tops with the coconut.

8. Bake for 20–23 minutes until the muffins are well risen and golden and the coconut is toasted. The tops will spring back when gently pressed.

9. Transfer to a wire rack to cool a little before eating.

Oat, apple and sunflower seed

We can thank my son Corin for these. He wanted me to make flapjacks and he asked me to add apple chunks and sunflower seeds. I know, it doesn't sound like a 12-year-old boy but that's what he wanted! After one taste of the finished flapjacks, I knew they would be perfect as muffins. And, of course, it's a simple way to get some good things into your children.

MAKES 12 MUFFINS

FOR THE BATTER
285 g/10 oz plain (all-purpose) flour
150 g/5 oz light muscovado sugar
2 tsp baking powder
¼ tsp salt
50 g/1¾ oz porridge oats
170 g/6 oz milk
2 eggs
100 g/3½ oz butter
50 g/1¾ oz golden (light corn) syrup

FOR THE FILLING
200 g/7 oz finely chopped unpeeled eating (dessert) apple
20 g/¾ oz sunflower seeds

FOR THE TOPPING
20 g/¾ oz jumbo oats
25 g/1 oz sunflower seeds
25 g/1 oz demerara sugar

1 Preheat the oven to 200°C/400°F/gas 6/fan oven 180°C. Grease and flour 12 muffin tin sections or line with paper liners.

2 Sift the flour, sugar, baking powder and salt into a large bowl, pushing the muscovado sugar through the sieve (strainer) with the back of a spoon. Stir in the porridge oats.

3 Combine the milk and eggs in a medium-sized bowl and mix well with a fork.

4 Melt the butter in a small bowl in the microwave or in a small saucepan. Stir the golden syrup into the melted butter and mix well.

5 Add all the wet ingredients to the dry, then fold the mixture together with a large metal spoon until just moistened. Fold in the chopped apple and sunflower seeds.

6 Spoon the batter into the prepared muffin tin sections.

7 For the topping, sprinkle the oats over evenly, then the sunflower seeds and finish with the sugar.

8 Bake for 20–22 minutes, until the muffins are well risen and golden and the tops spring back when gently pressed.

9 Transfer to a wire rack to cool a little before eating.

Peanut and muscovado sugar

The combination of light and dark muscovado sugar combined with the toasted peanuts in the batter gives the finished muffins a lovely depth of flavour, finished with a hint of vanilla. The muffins are beautifully moist, thanks to the ground nuts in the mixture, and contrast perfectly with the crunchy, nutty topping.

MAKES 11 MUFFINS

FOR THE BATTER
300 g/10$\frac{1}{2}$ oz plain (all-purpose) flour
$\frac{1}{8}$ tsp salt
100 g/3$\frac{1}{2}$ oz light muscovado sugar

1 tbsp baking powder
100 g/3$\frac{1}{2}$ oz raw peanuts, toasted (see page 10) and ground
170 g/6 oz milk
2 eggs
1 tsp vanilla essence (extract)

100 g/3$\frac{1}{2}$ oz butter
70 g/2$\frac{1}{2}$ oz dark muscovado sugar
FOR THE TOPPING
60 g/2 oz raw peanuts, toasted and roughly chopped
30 g/1 oz demerara sugar

1 Preheat the oven to 180°C/350°F/gas 4/fan oven 160°C. Grease and flour 11 muffin tin sections or line with paper liners.

2 Sift the flour, salt, light muscovado sugar and baking powder into a large bowl. You will need to push the light muscovado sugar through the sieve (strainer) with the back of a spoon.

3 Stir in the ground peanuts.

4 Combine the milk, eggs and vanilla in a medium-sized bowl and beat the ingredients together well with a fork.

5 Melt the butter in a small bowl in the microwave or in a small saucepan. Add the dark muscovado to the butter and stir well. There may be a few lumps of sugar in the mixture but don't worry.

6 Add the egg mixture and the melted butter mixture to the dry ingredients. Fold everything together until just combined.

7 Spoon the batter into the prepared muffin tin sections.

8 Sprinkle the tops evenly with chopped nuts, then the sugar.

9 Bake for 22–25 minutes until well risen and the muffins spring back when lightly pressed.

10 Transfer to a wire rack to cool a little before eating.

Pistachio, anise and almond

I was inspired to develop this muffin recipe after eating cantucci biscuits. These are traditional almond and honey biscuits from Tuscany in Italy, which are made to be dipped in vin santo, a sweet, golden dessert wine with a full-bodied and light flavour and slightly penetrating aroma.

MAKES 12 MUFFINS

FOR THE BATTER
8 g/1 tbsp anise seeds
1/8 tsp salt
310 g/11 oz plain (all-purpose) flour
170 g/6 oz caster (superfine) sugar

1 tbsp baking powder
60 g/2 oz ground almonds
170 g/6 oz milk
2 eggs
1 tsp almond essence (extract)
100 g/3½ oz butter

FOR THE FILLING AND TOPPING
100 g/3½ oz whole almonds, toasted (see page 10) and chopped
100 g/3½ oz pistachio nuts, roughly chopped
30 g/1 oz demerara sugar

1. Preheat the oven to 180°C/360°F/gas 4/fan oven 160°C. Grease and flour 12 muffin tin sections or line with paper liners.

2. Grind the anise with the salt using a pestle and mortar or in a nut grinder or a clean coffee grinder.

3. Sift the flour, sugar and baking powder into a large bowl. Stir in the ground anise and ground almonds.

4. Combine the milk, eggs and almond essence in a medium-sized bowl. Beat together thoroughly with a fork.

5. Melt the butter in a small bowl in the microwave or in a small saucepan.

6. Add the egg mixture and the melted butter to the dry ingredients and fold together with a large metal spoon until just combined. Fold in 70 g/2½ oz each of the toasted almonds and the pistachios. Chop the remaining nuts even finer.

7. Divide the batter evenly between the muffin tin sections.

8. Mix the remaining finely chopped nuts with the demerara sugar and sprinkle evenly over the muffins.

9. Bake for 22–25 minutes until well risen and the muffins spring back when lightly pressed.

10. Transfer to a wire rack to cool before eating.

Poppy seed and almond

This recipe makes delicious light muffins, which still have the lovely rich flavour of the ground almonds, with just a touch of citrus from the lemon to give them a bit of zest. They look beautiful, too, speckled with poppy seeds across the lovely lemon centre. Just look at that photograph. Doesn't that make you want to get baking?

MAKES 10 MUFFINS

FOR THE BATTER
310 g/11 oz plain (all-purpose) flour
170 g/6 oz caster (superfine) sugar
1 tbsp baking powder

⅛ tsp salt
50 g/1¾ oz ground almonds
40 g/1½ oz poppy seeds
Grated zest and juice of 1 lemon
A little milk
2 eggs

1 tsp almond essence (extract)
100 g/3½ oz butter
FOR THE TOPPING
50 g/1¾ oz flaked (slivered) almonds

1 Preheat the oven to 180°C/360°F/gas 4/fan oven 160°C. Grease and flour 10 muffin tin sections or line with paper liners.

2 Sift the flour, sugar, baking powder and salt into a large bowl. Stir in the ground almonds, poppy seeds and lemon zest.

3 Make up the lemon juice to 170 g/6 oz with milk. Combine with the eggs and almond essence in a medium-sized bowl. Beat together thoroughly with a fork.

4 Melt the butter in a small bowl in the microwave or in a small saucepan.

5 Add the egg mixture and the melted butter to the dry ingredients and fold together with a large metal spoon until just combined.

6 Divide the batter between the muffin tin sections and sprinkle evenly with the flaked almonds.

7 Bake for 23–25 minutes until golden and well risen and the muffins spring back when lightly pressed.

8 Transfer to a wire rack to cool a little before eating.

Rum and raisin

You will definitely taste the rum in these muffins, which were inspired by rum-and-raisin ice cream. There's lots of rum, lots of rum-soaked raisins and lots of cream, but unlike making ice cream, you don't have to wait ages and you can eat this popular flavour combination warm, in your fingers!

MAKES 12 MUFFINS

FOR THE FILLING
200 g/7 oz raisins
30 g/1 oz rum

FOR THE BATTER
310 g/11 oz plain (all-purpose) flour
170 g/6 oz light muscovado sugar
1 tbsp baking powder
1/8 tsp salt
100 g/3 1/2 oz butter

190 g/6 3/4 oz double (heavy) cream
100 g/3 1/2 oz dark rum
2 eggs

FOR THE TOPPING
40 g/1 1/2 oz demerara sugar

1 Soak the raisins in the rum for at least 1 hour.

2 Preheat the oven to 180°C/350°F/gas 4/fan oven 160°C. Grease and flour 12 muffin tin sections or line with paper liners.

3 Sift the dry batter ingredients into a large bowl and stir well. You will need to push the light muscovado sugar through the sieve (strainer) with a spoon.

4 Melt the butter in a small bowl in the microwave or in a small saucepan. Place the cream, rum and eggs in a medium-sized bowl and beat with a fork until just combined. Try not to thicken the cream.

5 Add the wet ingredients and the melted butter to the dry ingredients and gently fold together with a large metal spoon until just moistened.

6 Fold in the filling ingredients, including any rum that was not absorbed by the raisins. Spoon the batter into the sections of the prepared muffin tin.

7 Top the muffins with the demerara sugar.

8 Bake for about 20–22 minutes until well risen and golden and the tops of the muffins spring back when gently pressed.

9 Transfer to a wire rack to cool a little before eating.

Rum, cola and coconut

There is lots and lots of coconut in this superb muffin to complement the delicate flavour of the tender crumb and to contrast with the kick of the rum. Its layers really give a true taste of the Tropics – sweet, chewy coconut on the bottom of the muffin, rum-soaked coconut in the middle and toasted coconut on the top!

MAKES 12 MUFFINS

FOR THE CENTRE FILLING
60 g/2 oz sweetened desiccated (shredded) coconut
50 g/1³/₄ oz dark rum or Malibu

FOR THE BOTTOM FILLING
12 tsp/45 g sweetened desiccated coconut

FOR THE BATTER
310 g/11 oz plain (all-purpose) flour
1 tbsp baking powder
100 g/3¹/₂ oz light muscovado sugar
70 g/2¹/₂ oz caster (superfine) sugar

¹/₈ tsp salt
50 g/1³/₄ oz sweetened desiccated coconut
2 eggs
200 g/7 oz cola (not diet)
100 g/3¹/₂ oz butter

FOR THE TOPPING
50 g/1³/₄ oz sweetened desiccated coconut

1 Combine the centre filling ingredients and leave to soak for at least 1¹/₂ hours, preferably overnight.

2 Preheat the oven to 200°C/400°F/gas 6/fan oven 180°C.

3 Grease and flour 12 muffin tin sections or line with paper liners. For the bottom filling, place a teaspoon of sweetened shredded coconut in each muffin paper.

4 Into a large bowl, sift the flour, baking powder, sugars and salt. You will need to push the light muscovado sugar through the sieve (strainer) with the back of a spoon.

5 Stir the coconut into the flour.

6 In a medium-sized bowl, mix together the eggs and cola with a fork. Melt the butter in a small bowl in the microwave or in a small saucepan.

7 Add the egg and cola mixture and the melted butter to the flour mixture and fold together with a large metal spoon until just combined.

8 Spoon a little batter on top of the coconut in the bottom of each muffin section to cover it. Then place a teaspoon of the soaked rum and coconut filling on top of the batter in each muffin section. Share out all the filling evenly, including any leftover rum that wasn't absorbed. Top with the remaining batter.

9 Sprinkle the coconut for the topping evenly over the muffins and bake for 20–22 minutes until well risen and the tops spring back when gently pressed.

10 Transfer to a wire rack to cool a little before eating.

Sam's birthday peanut and cola

Sam is a good friend of mine who has the odd habit of putting salted peanuts in her cola. I tried this combo, and it is surprisingly good! (I have my own odd habit – I make some fresh popcorn and toss in some peanut M&Ms and ready-salted crisps while the popcorn is still hot.) I thought these muffins would make an original present, so here goes. Happy Birthday, Sam!

MAKES 10 MUFFINS

FOR THE BATTER
350 g/12¼ oz plain (all-purpose) flour
170 g/6 oz light muscovado sugar

2 tsp baking powder
⅛ tsp salt
190 g/6¾ oz cola (not diet)
100 g/3½ oz oil
2 eggs

FOR THE TOPPING
40 g/1½ oz demerara sugar
60 g/2 oz salted peanuts
10 'cola bottle' sweets (optional)

1 Preheat the oven to 180°C/350°F/gas 4/fan oven 160°C. Grease and flour 10 muffin tin sections or line with paper liners.

2 Sift the dry ingredients into a large bowl and stir well. You will need to push the light muscovado sugar through the sieve (strainer) with the back of a spoon.

3 Place the wet ingredients in a medium-sized bowl and beat with a fork until combined.

4 Add the wet ingredients to the dry ingredients and gently fold together with a large metal spoon until just moistened.

5 Spoon the batter into the prepared muffin tin sections.

6 Sprinkle first the peanuts and then the demerara sugar evenly over the tops of the muffins.

7 Bake for about 22–25 minutes until well risen and golden and the tops spring back when gently pressed.

8 Transfer to a wire rack to cool a little before eating. Decorate each muffin with one cola sweet, if liked.

Sweet cornmeal and peanut crumble

Unusual but very tasty, these definitely have an American feel to them. You can buy cornmeal in most large supermarkets now, though it is sometimes labelled as polenta, in which case you'll find it with the Italian-style ingredients. It has a lovely pale yellow colour and a distinctive texture that just goes perfectly with the peanut crumble topping.

MAKES 12 MUFFINS

FOR THE BATTER
200 g/7 oz plain (all-purpose) flour
100 g/3½ oz cornmeal
1 tbsp baking powder

⅛ tsp salt
100 g/3½ oz light muscovado sugar
100 g/3½ oz unsalted (sweet) butter
100 g/3½ oz clear honey
160 g/5½ oz milk
2 eggs

FOR THE TOPPING
50 g/1¾ oz unsalted butter, softened
80 g/3 oz plain (all-purpose) flour
30 g/1 oz cornmeal
20 g/¾ oz clear honey
20 g/¾ oz light muscovado sugar
50 g/1¾ oz raw peanuts, toasted (see page 10) and roughly chopped

1 Preheat the oven to 180°C/350°F/gas 4/fan oven 160°C. Grease and flour 12 muffin tin sections or line with paper liners.

2 Sift the dry batter ingredients into a large bowl, pushing the light muscovado sugar through the sieve (strainer) with the back of a spoon.

3 Melt the butter in a medium-sized bowl in the microwave or in a small saucepan. Add the honey, mix together and set aside.

4 Combine the milk and eggs in a medium-sized bowl, beat together with a fork.

5 Add the wet ingredients to the dry and gently fold together with a large metal spoon until just moistened. The batter may look a bit thin at first, but the cornmeal is very absorbent.

6 Spoon the batter evenly into the sections of the muffin tin.

7 Combine and rub together the topping ingredients in a small bowl. Sprinkle evenly over the muffins.

8   Bake for 20–22 minutes until well risen and
    golden and the tops spring back when gently
    pressed.

9   Transfer to a wire rack to cool a little before
    eating.

Sweet and spicy carrot and cream cheese

My husband Roger loves carrot cake and he asked me if I could do a sweet carrot muffin. The sweet cream cheese topping on carrot cake really makes it for me, but muffins are at their best warm, so a cold muffin spread with cream cheese icing seemed to defeat the object. The solution was simple – I put the sweet cream cheese in the middle!

MAKES 15 MUFFINS

FOR THE FIRST FILLING
170 g/6 oz carrots, grated
50 g/1³/₄ oz pecans, toasted (see page 10) and roughly chopped
50 g/1³/₄ oz sultanas (golden raisins)
40 g/1¹/₂ oz sweetened desiccated (shredded) coconut

FOR THE BATTER
300 g/10¹/₂ oz plain (all-purpose) flour
1 tbsp baking powder
170 g/6 oz light muscovado sugar
¹/₈ tsp salt
1 tsp ground cinnamon
¹/₂ tsp ground nutmeg (about 50 scrapes on a nutmeg grater)
¹/₈ tsp ground cloves
¹/₈ tsp ground allspice
2 eggs
185 g/6¹/₂ oz milk
100 g/3¹/₂ oz oil
1 tsp vanilla essence (extract)

FOR THE SECOND FILLING
135 g/4¹/₂ oz full-fat cream cheese
15 g/¹/₂ oz icing (confectioners') sugar

FOR THE TOPPING
20 g/³/₄ oz demerara sugar
30 g/1 oz sweetened desiccated coconut
70 g/2¹/₂ oz pecans, toasted and roughly chopped

1 Preheat the oven to 180°C/350°F/gas 4/fan oven 160°C. Grease and flour 15 sections of muffin tin or line with paper liners.

2 Prepare the first filling. Grate the carrots and place them in a medium bowl. Add in the pecans, sultanas and coconut and mix well.

3 Sift the flour, baking powder, sugar, salt, cinnamon, nutmeg, cloves and allspice into a large bowl. You will need to push the light muscovado sugar through the sieve (strainer) with the back of a spoon.

4 In a medium-sized bowl, beat together the eggs, milk, oil and vanilla with a fork.

5 Add the egg mixture to the flour mixture. Fold everything together, using a large metal spoon, until just combined. Then fold in the filling ingredients.

6 In a small bowl, work together the cream cheese and icing sugar. There's no need to sift the icing sugar, just stir the cream cheese and icing sugar with a rubber spatula, mashing and stirring until thoroughly mixed.

7 Spoon in just enough batter to cover the bottom of each of the muffin sections. Add half a tablespoon of cream cheese mixture to the centre of each muffin, then top with the remaining batter.

8 Mix the coconut and demerara sugar together in a small bowl. Sprinkle the chopped pecans evenly over the muffins, then add an even topping of the coconut and demerara.

9 Bake for 23–25 minutes until well risen and the tops spring back when gently pressed.

10 Transfer to a wire rack and leave to cool for 10 minutes before you eat them.

Toasted cashew nut

These muffins are golden, nutty, buttery and just beautiful! Cashew nuts have a rich, dense, delightfully strong flavour, which they can't help but impart to this muffin. Toasting the nuts really brings out that flavour and makes them taste even better, as well as adding even more fabulous, crunchy texture.

MAKES 12 MUFFINS

FOR THE BATTER
270 g/9½ oz plain (all-purpose) flour
1 tbsp baking powder
170 g/6 oz light muscovado sugar

⅛ tsp salt
100 g/3½ oz cashew nuts, toasted (see page 10) and ground
170 g/6 oz milk
2 eggs
100 g/3½ oz butter

FOR THE FILLING
100 g/3½ oz cashew nuts, toasted and chopped

FOR THE TOPPING
100 g/3½ oz whole cashew nuts

1 Preheat the oven to 200°C/400°F/gas 6/fan oven 180°C. Grease and flour 12 muffin tin sections or line with paper liners.

2 Sift the flour, baking powder, light muscovado sugar and salt into a large bowl. Use the back of a spoon to push the sugar through the sieve (strainer).

3 Stir in the ground cashew nuts.

4 Combine the milk and eggs in a medium-sized bowl and mix well with a fork.

5 Melt the butter in a small bowl in the microwave or in a small saucepan.

6 Add the wet ingredients to the dry. Fold together with a large metal spoon until just moistened.

7 Fold in the chopped cashew nuts.

8 Spoon the batter into the prepared sections of the muffin tin.

9 Sprinkle evenly with the whole cashew nuts.

10 Bake for 20–22 minutes, until the muffins are well risen and golden and the tops spring back when gently pressed.

11 Transfer to a wire rack to cool.

White chocolate, amaretto, almond and rhubarb

You know when you make something and then you come back to it and say to yourself, 'Did I make that?' That's how I feel about these muffins. They are absolutely delicious – although I think all my muffins are delicious! – but also very classy. Serve them on fine china plates to the guests you want to impress the most.

MAKES 12 MUFFINS

FOR THE BATTER
310 g/11 oz plain (all-purpose) flour
100 g/3½ oz caster (superfine) sugar
70 g/2½ oz light muscovado sugar
⅛ tsp salt

1 tbsp baking powder
60 g/2 oz ground almonds
120 g/4¼ oz milk
2 eggs
50 g/1¾ oz amaretto
100 g/3½ oz butter

FOR THE FILLING
200 g/7 oz rhubarb, chopped into
    5 mm/¼ in dice
150 g/5 oz white chocolate, roughly
    chopped
FOR THE TOPPING
50 g/1¾ oz flaked (slivered) almonds

1   Preheat the oven to 180°C/350°F/gas 4/fan oven 160°C. Grease and flour 12 muffin tin sections or line with paper liners.

2   Sift the flour, caster sugar, light muscovado sugar, salt and baking powder into a large bowl. You will need to push the light muscovado sugar through the sieve (strainer) with the back of a spoon.

3   Stir in the ground almonds.

4   Combine the milk, eggs, and amaretto in a medium-sized bowl, beating the ingredients together well with a fork.

5   Melt the butter in a small bowl in the microwave or in a small saucepan.

6   Add the wet ingredients to the dry ingredients and fold together until just combined.

7   Fold in the rhubarb and white chocolate.

8   Spoon the batter into the prepared sections of the muffin tin.

9   Sprinkle evenly with the topping.

10 Bake for 24–26 minutes until well risen and the muffins spring back when lightly pressed with a finger.

11 Transfer to a wire rack to cool before eating.

SAVOURY MUFFINS

Savoury muffins offer you the perfect excuse to eat muffins without the sense of guilt you sometimes get when you are eating cake! They're versatile too – you can enjoy them at any mealtime, either on their own, or paired with salad. You can serve them as a starter or just use them as bread.

The muffins in this section make use of meats, cheeses, chicken, fish and shellfish, and I've added a variety of herbs, pulses, vegetables and spices to create a colourful and very tasty selection of snacks and main-course recipes. I've also included several examples of sweet and savoury all rolled into one irresistible, harmonious taste experience. Bacon, Sweet Potato and Maple Syrup, Pear, Date and Stilton, Black pudding, Apple and Watercress, and Brie, Fig and Red Onion – just listing the recipe titles makes my tastebuds tingle!

Bacon, sweet potato and maple syrup

I find the combination of sweet and savoury flavours just irresistible and these sweet, tender, light muffins each have an utterly tempting bit of crisp bacon on the top. The recipe is very reminiscent of a traditional American breakfast, but these muffins are also perfect with your evening meal!

MAKES 14 MUFFINS

FOR THE BATTER
300 g/10½ oz smoked streaky bacon
100 g/3½ oz unsalted (sweet) butter
450 g/1 lb sweet potatoes

200 g/7 oz dark muscovado sugar
300 g/10½ oz plain (all-purpose) flour
1 tbsp baking powder
½ tsp salt
2 eggs
150 g/5 oz milk

50 g/1¾ oz maple syrup
FOR THE FILLING
14 tsp maple syrup

1   Take five rashers (slices) of bacon from the bacon for the filling. Cut these five into thirds and reserve for the topping. Chop the rest of the bacon.

2   Melt the unsalted butter in a frying pan over a medium heat. Fry the chopped bacon gently in the butter for 3–4 minutes, then set aside.

3   Preheat the oven to 200°C/400°F/gas mark 6/fan oven 180°C. Grease and flour 14 muffin tin sections or line with paper liners. Use a little extra oil or butter to grease the top of the muffin tin as well, as the maple syrup is very sticky.

4   Cook the sweet potatoes until tender. I find this easiest to do in the microwave (use your manufacture's booklet instructions for a jacket potato). Alternatively, bake them like jacket potatoes in the oven, or boil them in their skins, or peel and steam them. When the sweet potatoes are cooked, peel them, if necessary, and weigh out 250 g/8½ oz of the flesh, then use a fork to mash it together with the sugar. Allow the mixture to cool a little.

5   Sift the flour, baking powder and salt into a large bowl.

6   Place the eggs, milk and maple syrup in a medium-sized bowl and mix together thoroughly with a fork.

7 Add the sweet potato mixture to the flour, together with the egg mixture and the fried bacon and all the butter in the frying pan. Fold together with a large metal spoon until just combined.

8 Spoon in enough batter to half-fill the 14 prepared sections of the muffin tins. Place a generous teaspoon of maple syrup on top of the batter in each one, then share the remaining batter among all the muffin sections.

9 Place one piece of the reserved streaky bacon on the top of each muffin and then bake for 23–25 minutes until well risen and the tops spring back when gently pressed.

10 Transfer to a wire rack as quickly as you can, as any syrup that made its way up on to the top of the tin will become very sticky as it cools.

Black-eye bean and bacon

Black-eye beans (or black-eye peas, as they are often called) and bacon are made for each other, with the rich, buttery beans making a perfect contrast with the salty bacon. Add in a bit of piquancy from the spring onions and the hot sauce and you have a very tasty muffin.

MAKES 12 MUFFINS

FOR THE FILLING AND TOPPING
200 g/7 oz canned black-eye beans
250 g/8½ oz smoked streaky bacon
100 g/3½ oz butter

1 tsp hot pepper sauce
75 g/3 oz spring onions (scallions), finely sliced
Freshly ground black pepper, to taste
FOR THE BATTER
300 g/10½ oz plain (all-purpose) flour

1 tbsp baking powder
⅛ tsp salt
30 g/1 oz caster (superfine) sugar
10 g/3 tbsps chopped fresh parsley
2 eggs
185 g/6½ oz milk

1 Preheat the oven to 180°C/350°F/gas 4/fan oven 160°C. Grease and flour 12 muffin tin sections or line with paper liners.

2 Prepare the filling. Rinse and drain the canned black-eye beans. Melt the butter in a frying pan over a medium heat. Reserve four of the rashers of bacon for the topping and cut into thirds. Chop the remainder and place in the pan with the spring onions and fry for about 3–4 minutes until just cooked, then remove from the heat.

3 Add the hot pepper sauce to the bacon and spring onions. Season generously with freshly ground black pepper, stir well and set aside.

4 Make the batter. Sift the flour, baking powder, salt and sugar in a large bowl. Stir in the chopped parsley.

5 In a medium-sized bowl, beat together the eggs and milk with a fork.

6 Add the egg mixture and the contents of the frying pan to the flour mixture.

7 Using a large metal spoon, fold everything together until just combined, then fold in the black-eye beans.

8 Spoon the batter evenly into the sections of the muffin tin, top each with one of the reserved pieces of bacon and bake for 23–26 minutes until well risen and golden and the tops spring back when gently pressed.

9 Transfer to a wire rack and allow to cool a little before eating.

Black pudding, apple and watercress

This is a very moist muffin, packed full of exciting taste and interesting texture. In your mouth, each flavour asserts itself and you finish with a little peppery note from the mustard. They make a delicious snack on their own, or you can serve them as a lunch or supper dish, with a salad on the side.

MAKES 15 MUFFINS

FOR THE FILLING
40 g/1½ oz red onion, finely chopped
100 g/3½ oz butter
200 g/7 oz black pudding, chopped into
   5 mm/¼ in dice

100 g/3½ oz finely chopped unpeeled
   eating (dessert) apple
40 g/1½ oz watercress, roughly chopped
10 g/3 tbsp chopped fresh parsley
FOR THE BATTER
330 g/11½ oz plain (all-purpose) flour
1 tbsp baking powder

¼ tsp salt
½ tsp freshly ground black pepper
15 g/½ oz caster (superfine) sugar
5 g/1½ level tsp English mustard powder
2 eggs
185 g/6½ oz milk
150 g/5 oz full-fat crème fraîche

1   Preheat the oven to 180°C/350°F/gas 4/fan oven 160°C. Grease and flour 15 muffin tin sections or line with paper liners.

2   Prepare the filling. Over a medium heat, fry the chopped onion in the butter for 3–4 minutes until softened. Add the black pudding and the

chopped apple and fry for just 2 minutes – no longer, you are just trying to impart a bit of fried flavour to the black pudding and apple. Remove from the heat and stir in the chopped watercress and parsley, then set aside.

3   Make the batter. Sift the flour, baking powder, salt, black pepper, sugar and mustard powder into a large bowl. Tip in any black pepper that didn't go through the sieve (strainer).

4   In a medium-sized bowl, combine the eggs, milk and crème fraîche with a whisk.

5   Add the egg mixture and the contents of the frying pan to the flour mixture.

6   Using a large metal spoon, fold everything together until just combined.

7   Spoon the batter into the prepared sections of the muffin tin and bake for 23–26 minutes until well risen and golden and the tops spring back when gently pressed.

8   Transfer to a wire rack to cool a little before eating.

Brie, fig and red onion

An understated, creamy and slightly sweet muffin with an interesting combination of savoury flavours and a pleasing contrast of taste and texture from the figs. You don't need an overly ripe bit of cheese for this recipe – it is easier to prepare the cheese when it is firm, preferably straight from the fridge.

MAKES 12 MUFFINS

FOR THE FILLING
100 g/3½ oz butter
120 g/4½ oz finely chopped red onion
150 g/5 oz brie cheese

1 tbsp balsamic vinegar
150 g/5 oz ready-to-eat dried figs

FOR THE BATTER
300 g/10½ oz plain (all-purpose) flour
1 tbsp baking powder
½ tsp salt

30 g/1 oz light muscovado sugar
1 tsp freshly ground black pepper
2 eggs
185 g/6½ oz milk

1 Preheat the oven to 180°C/350°F/gas 4/fan oven 160°C. Grease and flour 12 muffin tin sections or line with paper liners.

2 Prepare the filling first. Melt the butter in a frying pan over a medium heat. Add the chopped onion and fry for about 3–4 minutes until just cooked. Remove from the heat, add the balsamic vinegar, stir well and allow to cool a little. Chop the cheese into 1 cm/½ cm cubes and quarter the figs.

3 Sift the flour, baking powder, salt, sugar and black pepper into a large bowl. Tip in any bits of black pepper that don't go through the sieve (strainer).

4 In a medium-sized bowl, beat together the eggs and milk with a fork.

5 Add the egg mixture along with the contents of the frying pan to the flour mixture. Use a spatula to scrape all the oniony butter out of the frying pan.

6 Using a large metal spoon, fold everything together until just combined, then fold in the brie and figs.

7 Spoon the batter into the prepared muffin tin and bake for 23–26 minutes until well risen and golden and the tops spring back when gently pressed.

8 Transfer to a wire rack and allow to cool a little before eating.

Carrot and coriander

These muffins taste really fresh and vegetable-sweet. Try them split and thickly spread with cream cheese, with a pile of grapes on the side. I also like to eat them with a handful of seaweed peanuts – the crisp seaweed-flavoured coating of the nuts, with just a hint of chilli or sesame, provides a perfect flavour complement.

MAKES 11 MUFFINS

FOR THE BATTER
300 g/10½ oz plain (all-purpose) flour
1 tbsp baking powder

15 g/½ oz caster (superfine) sugar
¼ tsp salt
1 tsp freshly ground black pepper
30 g/1 oz chopped fresh coriander
  (cilantro)

170 g/6 oz grated carrot
2 eggs
185 g/6½ oz milk
100 g/3½ oz oil

1 Preheat the oven to 180°C/350°F/gas 4/fan oven 160°C. Grease and flour 11 muffin tin sections or line with paper liners.

2 Into a large bowl, sift the flour, baking powder, sugar, salt and black pepper. Add to the bowl any black pepper that didn't go through the sieve (strainer). Using a large metal spoon, stir in the chopped coriander, then add in the grated carrot and mix well.

4 In a medium-sized bowl, beat together the eggs, milk and oil with a fork.

5 Add the egg mixture to the flour mixture. Fold everything together with a large metal spoon until just combined.

6 Spoon the batter into the prepared muffin tin sections.

7 Bake for 23–25 minutes until well risen and the tops spring back when gently pressed.

8 Transfer to a wire rack to cool a little before eating.

Fresh dill and cottage cheese

The cottage cheese provides a light, open-crumbed muffin with a lovely, moist texture. But inside these muffins, there's delicious flavour-packed surprise: sweet fried onions and the distinctive aniseed flavour of fresh dill! A couple of these and a crisp green salad will make a perfect light lunch.

MAKES 11 MUFFINS

FOR THE FILLING
100 g/3½ oz butter
50 g/1¾ oz finely chopped red onion

FOR THE BATTER
300 g/10½ oz plain (all-purpose) flour
1 tbsp baking powder
15 g/½ oz caster (superfine) sugar
¼ tsp salt
1 tsp freshly ground black pepper

10 g/about 2 tbsp chopped fresh dill (dill weed)
2 eggs
185 g/6½ oz milk
250 g/8½ oz cottage cheese

FOR THE TOPPING
11 small sprigs of fresh dill

1 Preheat the oven to 180°C/350°F/gas 4/fan oven 160°C. Grease and flour 11 muffin tin sections or line with paper liners.

2 Heat a frying pan over a medium heat, melt the butter and add the finely chopped red onion and fry for 3–4 minutes until softened and starting to go golden. Remove from the heat and set aside.

3 Sift the flour, baking powder, sugar, salt and black pepper into a large bowl, tipping in any black pepper that didn't go through the sieve (strainer). Add the chopped fresh dill and stir well.

4 In a medium-sized bowl, beat together the eggs, milk and cottage cheese with a fork. Add both the egg mixture and the contents of the frying pan to the flour mixture.

5 Using a large metal spoon, fold everything together until just combined.

6 Spoon the batter into the prepared muffin tin sections and top each muffin with a dill sprig.

7 Bake for 23–25 minutes until well risen and golden and the tops spring back when gently pressed.

8 Transfer to a wire rack to cool a little before eating.

Fresh pesto

These muffins have a really unusual appearance – they are a beautiful, pale green colour. They are also light, fresh, fragrant and full of flavour. Making the pesto for the muffins is very easy and very pleasing to do and all those fresh, fragrant flavours and colours from the pesto mixture carry through into the finished muffin.

MAKES 9 MUFFINS

FOR THE PESTO
20 g/³/₄ oz fresh basil leaves
120 g/4¹/₄ oz extra-virgin olive oil
50 g/1³/₄ oz pine nuts, toasted
  (see page 10)
2 garlic cloves, roughly sliced

1 tsp salt
40 g/1¹/₂ oz freshly grated Parmesan
  cheese
Freshly ground black pepper
FOR THE BATTER
300 g/10¹/₂ oz plain (all-purpose) flour
1 tbsp baking powder
30 g/1 oz caster (superfine) sugar

¹/₈ tsp salt
2 eggs
185 g/6¹/₂ oz milk
FOR THE TOPPING
15 g/¹/₂ oz extra-virgin olive oil
9 large fresh basil leaves
40 g/1¹/₂ oz freshly grated Parmesan
  cheese

1. Preheat the oven to 180°C/350°F/gas 4/fan oven 160°C. Grease and flour 9 muffin tin sections or line with paper liners.

2. Place all the pesto ingredients except the black pepper into a food processor and whizz until smooth. Season to taste with a few grinds of black pepper.

3. Sift the flour, baking powder, sugar and salt into a large bowl.

4. In a medium-sized bowl, beat the eggs and milk together with 200 g/7 oz of the fresh pesto.

5. Add the pesto mixture to the flour mixture.

6. Using a large metal spoon, fold everything together until just combined.

7. Spoon the batter evenly into the sections of the muffin tin. Sprinkle evenly with the Parmesan cheese. Dip a fresh basil leaf into the extra-virgin olive oil from the topping ingredients and then place the basil leaf on top of the cheese. When you have finished all the basil leaves, sprinkle any remaining olive oil over the muffins.

8 Bake for 20–23 minutes until well risen and golden and the tops spring back when gently pressed.

9 Transfer to a wire rack to cool a little before eating.

NOTE
Any remaining pesto can be stored in a small container. Drizzle a little extra olive oil over the top of the pesto and it will keep in the fridge for a week.

Goats' cheese and thyme

This is a simple, straight forward, yummy, savoury muffin; and like the others, it's great with a salad. I like to use chèvre blanc, *which is a French full-fat goats' cheese. It has a soft, edible rind that melts when cooked, so it doesn't have to be cut away before being added to the muffin mixture.*

MAKES 10 MUFFINS

FOR THE BATTER
300 g/10¹/₂ oz plain (all-purpose) flour
1 tbsp baking powder
15 g/¹/₂ oz caster (superfine) sugar

¹/₄ tsp salt
1 tsp freshly ground black pepper
5 g fresh thyme
2 eggs
185 g/6¹/₂ oz milk
100 g/3¹/₂ oz butter

FOR THE FILLING
200 g/7 oz goats' cheese, roughly chopped into 1 cm/¹/₂ in dice

FOR THE TOPPING
10 sprigs of fresh thyme

1 Preheat the oven to 180°C/350°F/gas 4/fan oven 160°C. Grease and flour 10 muffin tin sections or line with paper liners.

2 Sift the flour, baking powder, sugar, salt and black pepper into a large bowl. Tip in any black pepper that didn't go through the sieve (strainer). Strip the leaves from the thyme (don't worry about very soft stems, they can go in too), then roughly chop. Stir the thyme into the flour mixture.

3 In a medium-sized bowl, beat together the eggs and milk with a fork. Melt the butter in a small bowl in the microwave or in a small saucepan. Add both the egg mixture and the melted butter to the flour mixture.

4 Using a large metal spoon, fold everything together until just combined. Then gently fold in the chopped goats' cheese.

5 Spoon the batter into the prepared muffin tin sections and top each with a sprig of thyme.

6 Bake for 23–25 minutes until well risen and golden and the tops spring back when gently pressed.

7 Transfer to a wire rack to cool before eating.

Hummus

These are very tasty savoury muffins on their own, but they really come into their own as an accompaniment to curries. I like to serve these with keema mattar *– a Indian dish of minced meat, fresh peas and yoghurt, flavoured with chilli, turmeric, fresh coriander, garlic, ginger and garam masala.*

MAKES 12 MUFFINS

FOR THE HUMMUS
410 g/15 oz can of chick peas garbanzos, rinsed and drained
2 garlic cloves, roughly chopped
1 tsp ground cumin
30 g/1 oz lemon juice

50 g/1³/₄ oz tahini paste
95 g/3¹/₂ oz extra-virgin olive oil
³/₄ tsp salt
¹/₄ tsp freshly ground black pepper
FOR THE BATTER
300 g/10¹/₂ oz plain (all-purpose) flour
1 tbsp baking powder

15 g/¹/₂ oz caster (superfine) sugar
¹/₄ tsp salt
1 tsp freshly ground black pepper
1 tsp ground cumin
2 eggs
185 g/6¹/₂ oz milk
100 g/3¹/₂ oz extra-virgin olive oil

1   Preheat the oven to 180°C/350°F/gas 4/fan oven 160°C. Grease and flour 12 muffin tin sections or line with paper liners.

2   Place all the hummus ingredients in the food processor and whizz to a smooth purée.

3   Sift the flour, baking powder, sugar, salt, black pepper and ground cumin into a large bowl. Tip in any pepper remaining in the sieve (strainer).

4   Beat together the eggs, milk and extra-virgin olive oil with a fork. Weigh out 200 g/7 oz of the hummus and then beat into the egg mixture.

5   Add the egg and hummus mixture to the flour mixture. Use a large metal spoon and fold everything together until just combined.

6   Spoon the batter evenly into the muffin tin sections and bake for 23–26 minutes until well risen and golden and the tops spring back when gently pressed.

7   Transfer to a wire rack to cool before eating.

NOTE
The hummus mixture makes enough for two batches of muffins but you can just serve the extra portion with the muffins themselves if you like. You can also use shop-bought hummus, in which case you should add an extra ¹/₂ tsp of ground cumin to the flour mixture. It is not hard to make the hummus yourself, however, and it does taste so much nicer!

Peanut butter, chilli, coriander and chicken

Yes, really – chicken muffins! And very good they are too, especially cooled to room temperature, when you can fully appreciate the complex savoury flavour of the muffin and the cold, juicy chunks of chicken. I find the little mini chicken fillets sold now in supermarkets the easiest to use for this recipe, but you can use chopped chicken breast or even thigh meat.

MAKES 12 MUFFINS

FOR THE BATTER
Finely grated zest and juice of 1 lime
70 g/2½ oz oil
50 g/1¾ oz finely chopped red onion
400 g/14 oz chicken breast or thigh meat, cut into 1 cm/½ in dice

1 large fat red chilli, seeded and finely chopped
1 garlic clove, finely chopped
1 tsp dried shrimp paste
50 g/1¾ oz crunchy peanut butter
20 g/3 tbsp chopped fresh coriander (cilantro)
300 g/10½ oz plain (all-purpose) flour

1 tbsp baking powder
⅛ tsp salt
30 g/1 oz light muscovado sugar
2 eggs
185 g/6½ oz coconut milk

1 Preheat the oven to 180°C/350°F/gas 4/fan oven 160°C. Grease and flour 12 muffin tin sections or line with paper liners. Put the lime zest into a large bowl.

2 Place the oil in a frying pan over a medium heat. Fry the chopped onion for 2 minutes and then add the chicken. Fry the chicken for 3 minutes over a medium heat until all the chicken turns white and is nearly cooked through. Add the chilli, garlic and dried shrimp paste, then fry for 2 minutes.

3 Add the peanut butter to the frying pan and allow it to melt. Remove the pan from the heat, squeeze in the juice of the lime, then add the chopped coriander and stir well. Leave the mixture to cool while you prepare the dry ingredients.

4 Sift the flour, baking powder, salt and light muscovado sugar into the large bowl with the lime zest. You will need to push the sugar through the sieve (strainer) with the back of a spoon. Stir well.

5   In a medium-sized bowl, beat together the eggs and coconut milk with a fork. (Coconut milk can become a bit solid in the can, so give it a good shake before you open it, and then a really good stir with a fork once it's open.)

6   Add the egg mixture and the contents of the frying pan to the flour mixture.

7   Using a large metal spoon, fold everything together until just combined.

8   Spoon the batter into the prepared muffin tin sections and bake for 23–25 minutes until well risen and golden and the tops spring back when gently pressed.

9   Transfer to a wire rack and allow to cool a little before eating.

Pear, date and stilton

The pear is a subtle flavour in this muffin but it provides a well-rounded sweetness that is accentuated by the dates and in perfect counterpoint with the stronger, slightly salty flavour of the blue cheese. These muffins are wonderfully versatile — you could eat them as a snack or a light lunch with salad, or even add them to your cheeseboard at dinner.

MAKES 11 MUFFINS

FOR THE BATTER
340 g/12 oz plain (all-purpose) flour
170 g/6 oz caster (superfine) sugar
1 tbsp baking powder
$\frac{1}{8}$ tsp salt
220 g/7$\frac{1}{2}$ oz drained canned pears
100 g/3$\frac{1}{2}$ oz oil
2 eggs

FOR THE FILLING
50 g/1$\frac{3}{4}$ oz ready-to-eat dates, chopped
70 g/2$\frac{1}{2}$ oz Stilton cheese, crumbled
50 g/1$\frac{3}{4}$ oz walnuts, roughly chopped

FOR THE TOPPING
50 g/1$\frac{3}{4}$ oz walnuts, roughly chopped

1   Preheat the oven to 200°C/400°F/gas 6/fan oven 180°C. Grease and flour 11 muffin tin sections or line with paper liners.

2   Sift the flour, sugar, baking powder and salt into a large bowl and stir well.

3   Whizz the drained pears in a blender or food processor, then use a rubber spatula to scrape the purée into a medium-sized bowl.

4   Add the oil and eggs to the puréed pears and beat together with a fork.

5   Add the wet ingredients to the dry, and fold together with a large metal spoon until just moistened.

6   Gently fold in the dates, Stilton cheese and the walnuts.

7   Spoon the batter into the prepared muffin tin sections.

8   Sprinkle the chopped walnuts evenly over the top.

9   Bake for 22–24 minutes, until the muffins are well risen and a deep golden. The tops will spring back when gently pressed with a finger.

10 Transfer to a wire rack to cool a little before eating.

Pepperoni and sun-dried tomato pizza

This muffin recipe includes some classic pizza topping ingredients; pepperoni, onions, garlic, anchovies, extra-virgin olive oil, Mozzarella cheese, Parmesan cheese, black olives, sun-dried tomatoes and oregano! You even get the pizza experience of melting, stringy cheese when you pull the warm muffins apart.

MAKES 12 MUFFINS

100 g/3½ oz extra-virgin olive oil
75 g/3 oz finely chopped red onion
1 garlic clove, grated on a microplane grater
2 anchovies, chopped
100 g/3½ oz pepperoni slices
FOR THE BATTER
300 g/10½ oz plain (all-purpose) flour
1 tbsp baking powder

15 g/½ oz caster (superfine) sugar
¼ tsp salt
1 tsp freshly ground black pepper
2 tsp dried oregano or 2 tbsp fresh chopped oregano
2 eggs
185 g/6½ oz milk
FOR THE FILLING
75 g/3 oz sun-dried tomatoes, roughly chopped
50 g/1¾ oz sliced black olives

150 g/5 oz grated Mozzarella cheese
50 g/1¾ oz freshly grated Parmesan cheese
FOR THE TOPPING
50 g/1¾ oz grated Mozzarella cheese
35 g/1¼ oz freshly grated Parmesan cheese
Fresh or dried oregano
Freshly ground black pepper
Sun-dried tomato oil from the jar of tomatoes

1   Preheat the oven to 180°C/350°F/gas 4/fan oven 160°C. Grease and flour 12 muffin tin sections or line with paper liners.

2   Put the extra-virgin olive oil in a frying pan over a medium heat. Add the finely chopped onion and fry for 3 minutes or until just softened. Add the grated garlic and chopped anchovies and fry for a minute or so until the anchovies melt. Remove from the heat and set aside to cool a little.

3   Cut six slices of the pepperoni into halves and reserve for the topping. Chop the remainder.

4   Sift the flour, baking powder, sugar, salt and pepper into a large bowl. Tip in any black pepper that doesn't go through the sieve (strainer), then stir in the oregano.

5   In a medium-sized bowl, beat together the eggs and milk with a fork.

6   Add the egg mixture along with the contents of the frying pan to the flour mixture. Use a spatula to get all the olive oil out of the frying pan.

7   Using a large metal spoon, fold everything together until just combined.

8   Put the chopped pepperoni into a bowl with all the other filling ingredients and then gently fold all the filling ingredients into the muffin batter. Be careful not to over-mix.

9   Spoon the batter into the prepared muffin tin sections. Top the muffins with the mixed cheeses, half a slice of pepperoni, a sprinkle of dried or fresh oregano and a grinding of black pepper. Drizzle ½ tsp of sun-dried tomato oil over each muffin.

10   Bake for 23–25 minutes until well risen and golden and the tops spring back when gently pressed.

11   Transfer to a wire rack to cool a little before eating, but do serve them warm!

Prawn with fresh chives

The flavour, the colour, the textures…! Never mind making prawn cocktail and stuffing it into little puff pastry cases, or even prawn sandwiches, make these – they are fantastic! Don't serve them too warm – I think these are at their best when they have cooled almost to room temperature.

MAKES 11 MUFFINS

FOR THE BATTER
330 g/11½ oz plain (all-purpose) flour
1 tbsp baking powder
15 g/½ oz caster (superfine) sugar
¼ tsp salt
1 tsp freshly ground black pepper
20 g fresh chives, finely chopped or
  snipped with scissors
2 eggs
130 g/4½ oz milk

150 g/5 oz full-fat crème fraîche
50 g/1¾ oz tomato ketchup (catsup)
100 g/3½ oz butter
FOR THE FILLING
300 g/10½ oz cooked peeled prawns
  (shrimp), thawed if frozen

1. Preheat the oven to 200°C/400°F/gas 6/fan oven 180°C. Grease and flour 11 muffin tin sections or line with paper liners.

2. Sift the flour, baking powder, sugar, salt and pepper into a large bowl. Tip in any pepper that doesn't go through the sieve (strainer). Stir in the chives.

3. In a medium-sized bowl, whisk together the eggs, milk, crème fraîche and ketchup. Melt the butter in a small bowl in the microwave or in a small saucepan.

4. Add the egg mixture and the melted butter to the flour mixture. Using a large metal spoon, fold everything together until just combined.

5. Squeeze the prawns to remove excess moisture and pat dry on kitchen paper (paper towels). Gently fold the prawns into the muffin batter.

6. Spoon the batter into the prepared muffin tin sections; the sections will be very full.

7. Bake for 23–25 minutes until well risen and golden and the tops spring back when gently pressed.

8. Transfer to a wire rack to cool a little before eating.

Smoked mackerel, courgette, tomato, olive and fresh basil

These are a meal in themselves – you have fish, vegetable and muffin all in one – and they are equally delicious hot or cold. The grated courgettes make the muffins very moist and their green flecks look very attractive, contrasting with the red sun-blush tomatoes and black olives.

MAKES 12 MUFFINS

FOR THE FILLING
100 g/3½ oz grated courgette (zucchini)
75 g/3 oz sun-blush tomatoes, halved
40 g/1½ oz sliced black olives

150 g/5 oz smoked mackerel, skinned and torn into small chunks
15 g/3 heaped tbsp torn or roughly chopped fresh basil

FOR THE BATTER
300 g/10½ oz plain (all-purpose) flour
1 tbsp baking powder

15 g/½ oz caster (superfine) sugar
¼ tsp salt
1 tsp freshly ground black pepper
2 eggs
185 g/6½ oz milk
100 g/3½ oz extra-virgin olive oil

1 Preheat the oven to 180°C/350°F/gas 4/fan oven 160°C. Grease and flour 12 muffin tin sections or line with paper liners.

2 Put the grated courgette into a medium-sized bowl with the rest of the prepared filling ingredients. Mix well.

3 Sift the flour, baking powder, sugar, salt and black pepper into a large bowl. Tip in any black pepper that doesn't go through the sieve (strainer).

4 In a medium-sized bowl, beat together the eggs, milk and olive oil with a fork. Add the egg mixture to the flour mixture and fold everything together with a large metal spoon until just combined.

5 Gently fold in all the filling ingredients.

6 Spoon the muffin batter into the prepared muffin tin sections.

7 Bake for 23–25 minutes until well risen and golden and the tops spring back when gently pressed.

8 Transfer to a wire rack to cool a little before eating.

Smoked oyster, buckwheat and chives

The buckwheat flour in the muffins provides wonderful colour and a rich earthy flavour, which holds its own and works beautifully with the strong smokiness of the oysters. Crème fraîche provides just the right acidic, sour note and the chives round everything off with a slight oniony flavour.

MAKES 12 MUFFINS

FOR THE BATTER
200 g/7 oz plain (all-purpose) flour
100 g/3¹/₂ oz buckwheat flour
1 tbsp baking powder

15 g/¹/₂ oz caster (superfine) sugar
¹/₄ tsp salt
1 tsp freshly ground black pepper
20 g fresh whole chive stalks
2 eggs
185 g/6¹/₂ oz milk

150 g/5 oz full-fat crème fraîche
100 g/3¹/₂ oz unsalted (sweet) butter
FOR THE FILLING
2 x 85 g/3¹/₄ oz cans of smoked oysters in oil, drained and halved

1 Preheat the oven to 180°C/350°F/gas 4/fan oven 160°C. Grease and flour 12 muffin tin sections or line with paper liners.

2 Sift the flours, baking powder, sugar, salt and black pepper into a large bowl. Tip in any black pepper that didn't go through the sieve (strainer). Reserve 12 of the chive stalks for topping. Chop or snip the remainder and stir into the mixture.

3 In a medium-sized bowl, whisk together the eggs, milk and crème fraîche. Melt the unsalted butter in a small bowl in the microwave or in a small saucepan.

4 Add the egg mixture and the melted butter to the flour mixture, fold everything together with a large metal spoon until just combined.

5 Gently fold the halved oysters into the muffin batter. Spoon the batter into the prepared muffin tin sections. Tie each of the whole reserved chives into a knot and place one on top of each muffin, pressing down gently.

6 Bake for 23–25 minutes until well risen and golden and the tops spring back when gently pressed.

7 Transfer to a wire rack to cool a little before eating.

Tuna, celery, spring onion, apple and pecan

A super-healthy combination of apple, vegetables, tuna and toasted pecans goes into this fantastic muffin. Chop all the vegetables very finely – the celery in particular – and you will be rewarded with a fresh and tasty muffin, perfect for lunch, supper or an 'any time' snack.

MAKES 13 MUFFINS

FOR THE FILLING

1 x 185 g/6½ oz can of tuna in brine or spring water, drained

130 g/4½ oz finely chopped unpeeled eating (dessert) apple

60 g/2 oz very finely chopped celery

60 g/2 oz finely sliced spring onion (scallion)

50 g/1¾ oz pecan nuts, toasted (see page 10) and roughly chopped

FOR THE BATTER

300 g/10½ oz plain (all-purpose) flour

1 tbsp baking powder

½ tsp salt

1 tsp freshly ground black pepper

⅛ tsp paprika

15 g/½ oz caster (superfine) sugar

2 eggs

185 g/6½ oz milk

100 g/3½ oz butter

1 Preheat the oven to 180°C/350°F/gas 4/fan oven 160°C. Grease and flour 13 muffin tin sections or line with paper liners. Mix all the filling ingredients together well in a bowl.

2 Sift the flour, baking powder, salt, black pepper, paprika and sugar into a large bowl. Tip back in any black pepper that didn't go through the sieve (strainer).

3 In a medium-sized bowl, beat together the eggs and milk with a fork. Melt the butter in a small bowl in the microwave or in a small saucepan.

4 Add the egg mixture and the melted butter to the flour mixture.

5 Using a large metal spoon, fold everything together until just combined. Gently fold the filling ingredients into the muffin batter.

6 Spoon the batter into the prepared muffin tin sections and bake for 23–26 minutes until well risen and golden and the tops spring back when gently pressed.

7 Transfer to a wire rack to cool a little before eating.

Wholemeal with muscovado sugar

Although these have a sweet flavour, they also work well as a savoury muffin, so I've included them in this section. They are ideal for spreading with butter or jam but they also go really well with a slab of your favourite cheese for tea or an afternoon snack. You could try them with soup or salad, too.

MAKES 10 MUFFINS

FOR THE BATTER
300 g/10½ oz wholemeal bread flour

⅛ tsp salt
1 tbsp baking powder
185 g/6½ oz milk
2 eggs

100 g/3½ oz butter
185 g/6½ oz dark muscovado sugar
FOR THE TOPPING
40 g/1½ oz demerara sugar

1 Preheat the oven to 200°C/400°F/gas 6/fan oven 180°C. Grease and flour 10 muffin tin sections or line with paper liners.

2 Sift the flour, salt and baking powder into a large bowl. Add back into the bowl all the bran that was sieved out of the wholemeal flour.

3 Combine the milk and eggs in a medium-sized bowl and beat together with a fork.

4 Melt the butter in a medium-sized bowl in the microwave or in a small saucepan. Add the dark muscovado sugar to the melted butter and mix well with a fork.

5 Add the wet ingredients to the dry ingredients and fold everything together with a large metal spoon until just moistened.

6 Spoon into the prepared muffin tin sections. Sprinkle the demerara sugar evenly over the tops.

7 Bake for about 18–20 minutes until well risen and the tops of the muffins spring back when gently pressed.

8 Transfer to a wire rack to cool a little before eating.

Index